The Organized Thinker

LESLEY GELLER

Copyright © 2020 Lesley Geller
All rights reserved.

ISBN 13: 9798668153855

*How to think and produce like an organized person.
Even with a messy desk.*

TABLE OF CONTENTS

	Acknowledgments	vii
1	My Journey	1
2	Being Present	2
3	Put It Down	4
4	Planning as a Way of Thinking	8
5	Investing in the Plan. Not the Outcome	13
6	Organization and Structure = Success	17
7	Secure the Base Now; Secure your Wealth Later	19
8	Mess Causes Stress	21
9	The Easy Stuff. That's always the Hardest to Find	23
10	Life-Changing Morning Rituals	28
11	Work from Home Organization	32
12	Organizing Mail	37
13	Organizing Our Thoughts through Breathing	39
14	The Calendar	42
15	So Many Shoes	49
16	The Garage	53
17	Rethinking the To-Do List	56
18	Fine-Tuning the Daily List	60
19	Increase Your Bottom Line	63
20	Your Health and Negative Thinking	67
21	Accountability	71
22	Business Systems	75
23	Procrastination	79
24	Schedule Scrupulously	84
25	Office Organization	87
26	Eliminate E-mail Overload	92
27	Sustainability	97
	About the Author	101

ACKNOWLEDGMENTS

This book is dedicated to my mom, the most organized thinker I have yet to meet, and to my home team that has encouraged me to be a player on the field of my life. Without my home team, I would not be able to contribute to the lives of others in the way I do. I thank you for being my smile, my laughter, my shoulder, and my main support.

Life is so much better with all of you in it.

And to my clients who are constantly pushing themselves to the next level, inspiring me to continue searching for my best self as well. You amaze me with your talents, courage, and endless perseverance. Keep moving those feet, and when you get stuck, remember that the best way to start anything is to begin.

Why should you become an organized thinker?
Maybe you have never been the one to consistently make your bed, keep the kitchen counter clean, or have a desk free of clutter. Yet do you secretly wish you could? Does the mere thought of trying to get your inbox down to just fifty e-mails make you want to get rid of your computer completely?

Do you really want to just start from here—where your reality is a messy desk with piles of paper layered with unknown business—and just clean your slate so you can start afresh?

Perfect. You have come to just the right spot.

The sweet spot in being an organized and clutter-free person, who has time to complete their daily tasks, as well as having time to regroup and be calm, is right here, and it's not about becoming something you are not. Maybe having life clutter free does not come to you easily. Maybe continuously trying to figure out where things should be kept is not organic for you. No problem. Because the sweet spot—the spot where humans find actual sustainable success—does not stem from how they align their things, but instead, it stems from how they align their thinking.

With some simple yet practical techniques, tried and tested on all age groups and all educational backgrounds, this book will help you in gaining access to what you have been most craving. Organization from the inside . . . out.

All you need is an open mind and a willingness to believe that you can achieve what you want. With fifteen years of experience in the business, I have seen what works and what doesn't, and have had the pleasure of experiencing real and sustainable change in the way people think and therefore do.

In this book, you will learn:

- How to think like an organized person.
- How to compartmentalize your thinking as well as what you do.
- How to stay motivated day after day.
- How to design projects in a way that entices you to complete them.
- How to transform a bad day into a great day.

- How to reap the rewards of an organized person, even if you are not one.
- How to create daily, weekly, and monthly tasks, eliminating all stress surrounding them.
- How to be a finisher for every project and task at hand.
- How to turn problems into puzzles.
- How to transform negative thinking into positive thinking.
- How to put a box around all thoughts and things, so that every single thing in your life is easy to manage.

Before we begin to dig into how an organized person actually thinks, we need to first dig into this whole notion of organization. Let's take a look at how we operate personally, in addition to as a society, so that we can look deeply at our own relationship with organization.

People around the world are struggling universally with organization to accomplish their goals. They come from different socio-cultural backgrounds—from different age groups, income levels, education levels and religions. In fact, it appears that as our society becomes more and more adept with technological advances, our ability to organize appears to be suffering even more.

How can that be?

I mean, the very core of what drives so many technological advances today are meant to help the average person become more organized, not less! Phones that fit in our pockets and hold basically the most important aspects of our life—from simple things like contact details of everyone we know and even those we don't. It has altered the way people work, socialize, organize, and entertain themselves. Our hourly, monthly, and yearly calendar of events reminds us with alarms that even add specific locations as to where they will take place. How is it that we are still showing up late or forgetting events altogether?

Technology has advanced to such an extent that now we can have access to online banking to check our accounts, transfer money, and pay bills by sitting at home. We can check the weather, so we know what to expect for the day; check our e-mail while on the train, a bus, or waiting in line at Starbucks; access our favorite songs, allowing us to play music at the click of a button without any other devices; keep track of our exercise for the day; carry notes and receive reminders about when we need to stand up (have we gotten that pathetic that we don't know when we have been sitting too long?); we have GPS to direct us to our destinations, a map, and even a human voice telling us how to get to our next spot . . . And that is just the beginning, right?

It might be faster for me to list what we CAN'T do with the phone in our hand.

But wait, there is much more!

You can shop for houses on sale, check on your stocks, listen to a few podcasts, and watch a movie or the latest series you missed last night . . . all on your way to work on the train. And yet, I have still barely skimmed the surface!

Busy entrepreneurs can check social media to keep up with the lives of people they love, those that they don't, and also constantly assess their own lives to see if they are keeping up! You can create social media posts to help market your business and follow others to gain more followers, because, of course, we want everyone following us! You can even keep a close eye on LinkedIn and keep up with connections you have made—their work anniversaries, new jobs, promotions they have received, and who exactly is checking out your profile.

I am exhausted from just creating this list of things we can access on a device, which is just the size of a wallet! It is not surprising that we are physically and mentally addicted to this device.

I am not sure what is more surprising . . . how a tiny object can be responsible for so many aspects of our life, or that, in spite of everything we seemingly need in one spot, we continue on this path of disorganization and stay completely overwhelmed.

Disorganization:
Noun; lack of proper planning control; inability to plan one's activities or affairs efficiently.

It many ways it seems completely unreasonable that we are not able to plan properly and are lacking discipline, when everything is literally at our finger tips, doesn't it? Or does it actually make perfect sense?

Fact: Clutter causes stress and anxiety.

But what you may not know is that clutter isn't just physical. It is also mental, emotional, spiritual, or digital. The thousands of unanswered e-mails, work scattered across the desk, dozens of open tabs on the internet browser, and even unused clothes and items that just collect dust are examples of the clutter in your life that cause stress and anxiety. The harder you try to stop new clutter from coming in, the more stressed, anxious, and overwhelmed you feel. It becomes a vicious cycle.

In 2012, researchers at the Yale School of Medicine discovered that the two parts of your brain associated with conflict and pain, the anterior cingulate cortex and insula, overact whenever you try to let go of possessions that you're emotionally connected to. The stronger the emotional connection to the time, the more painful it becomes and the harder it is to let go.

—"Mental Health" by Mayo Oshin

Clutter physically represents a to-do list.

This goes a long way to explaining about a society that is overwhelmed, self-medicating to fall asleep at night, and getting prescriptions for everything under the sun. Many have this sinking feeling that they are falling apart at the seams and they resort to everything possible to escape this thing we call life.

1

MY JOURNEY

As a retired teacher, spending hours with some of the brightest third, fourth, and fifth grade math students in our district, a mother of four amazing emerging adults, and a Business and Life Coach for almost fifteen years, I have watched stress levels sky rocket.

I have witnessed seven-year-olds tell me about their dreams to attend Ivy League colleges, eight-year-olds cry because they didn't get a 100 percent (even though we don't give letter grades in our school), emerging adults tell me they are getting all As but are so stressed out that they are popping pills to compensate for the lack of sleep and anxiety, and entrepreneurs admit that they can't fall asleep without medication.

When asked the question: "At what time of day do you find you are the most anxious?" a successful professional replied, "When I first open my eyes in the morning."

I raised four beautiful, talented, bright, athletic children and I can honestly say that I have seen stress hiding in every corner, with a clear understanding that none of us are safe from the repercussions of our lack of organization.

2

BEING PRESENT

To be organized, mind, body, and spirit is to achieve the ultimate goal of human beings—the ability to be present.

When we are truly present, in our body, life, relationships and work, we become powerful human beings. We awake each day with a sense of calm and can breathe easily, inhaling and exhaling at the exact same slow pace. When we are present, we become aware of our own steady heartbeat. In this state, we are given back the power in our life. We know where we are, where we want to go next, and are able to access our tools easily at a minute's notice.

It begins with the way we think.

This book is what everyone needs. It's about tidying up all the parts of your life so that everything is in a place that makes sense, not only so you can find it easily, but so that you don't have to think about it when it isn't needed.

Imagine if we could compartmentalize everything so that at any given moment, that moment would be the only thing to focus on. Imagine the ability to be present in a way that would allow you to truly only think about one thing at a time.

It's not only possible, but you can actually attain that just as you are today. Just who you are today. The only shift will be in tapping into that sweet spot of how you think. It's about being mindful and present enough to understand that, as we stand still in this moment, we needn't worry about what will come next. It is about the possibility that all the things listed as 'next,' are carefully compartmentalized and will arrive as they should, when they should, at a time that you have already arranged.

This is the sweet spot.

Think of it as having a specific box for every compartment in your life. A specific spot. We could put your emotions, fears, enthusiasm, even your to-do list, in the box. But not just any box. It is a box that you never had to think about unless you were about to grab the contents out of it. A box that would present itself only when needed. A box that freed up space in your mind on an hourly basis so that you could be mindful about the moment you are/were in. Think of it like the cloud, the safety net of knowing everything is safe. Except this cloud is not the one on your phone; it is the one in your mind.

I bet you can't imagine that. I bet you have no idea what I am even talking about, because the concept seems so unreal. After all, you have your phone, which is storing basically your whole life in one spot. Right?

Wrong.

Technology, the very thing created to make our life easier, has done just the opposite. What began as helpful and timely, has turned into something we just can't put down. And to make matters worse, instead of making us more efficient, we have become obsessed with all that technology has to offer and, in exchange, we have become less focused and more overwhelmed.

3

PUT IT DOWN

If we had a box, we could put it in there. But if not, maybe we could just put it down.

I believe the biggest part of the problem is that we are now carrying our most precious belongings in this tiny object that seems to offer security. How could we put it down?

How do we now knowingly put this device down that we have come to depend on, rely on for dates, times, arrangements, calls, schedules, weather, contact details, e-mails . . . everything we need all day long?

How do we now put it down?

We have become the reliable go-to person, with people counting on us to respond to texts, calls, and e-mails any hour of the day. How can we possibly just turn it off? What will we say? What will be our reason? Our excuse?

The days when we were simply not home have been long gone. Now people question the silence, asking, "Why aren't you picking up?"

We know how much you are on the phone. We see you at every street corner, coffee shop, and everywhere you go . . . on the phone. We have no idea if you are looking for your latest playlist or checking your e-mails, but we know for sure that you are looking at that device and that surely you SAW my name flash across the screen even if you chose not to answer it. Even if you chose to turn the ringer off, you saw it and could have responded with something. We are on to you . . .

Right? That is how the conversation goes when you don't answer the call before voice mail picks up, text back in a millisecond, or e-mail back within the half hour. We are all onto each other because we are all doing it ourselves and it is driving all of us crazy!

It doesn't seem to matter which side of the fence you are standing on. If you are the one waiting for the call back or waiting for a single text response, your whole day could be affected in trying to figure out why in the world you are not getting a response. Yet if you are on the other side, trying to manage the over stimulation of friends, family, and co-workers, your brain feels so busy that sometimes you just can't bear to respond.

The more you resist, the more it persists.

The thing is that you just need to put it down! That's right. Let go of the conversation that the world, in fact, might end if we are not as responsive as possible. AS if every text, phone call, and text is about to be someone's last call for help.

The more we continue to have a 24x7 mentality about responding to people, regardless of whether it is work, family, or friend related, the more we will need to continue. We need to let go of our expectation that others will respond 24x7 as well, because that is the only way that we can stop this vicious cycle. We need to stop exaggerating our sense of importance, as well as the importance of others.

If you can quiet the voices in your head for just a moment, you may see that most things people consider urgent, are not urgent at all. Not. At. All.

I can already hear where you are going next as you read this, because as a coach, I have heard it all!

You haven't met my children. You have no idea . . .
Not in the job I have. That would never work . . .

People in my life would freak out. They would send out a search party . . .
My husband would never survive . . .
My daughter always has some crisis going on . . . I need to be available.
Not after what happened last time with my son. No way!

Trust me, I hear you. I empathize with you and I can even admit that I too believed that at one point in my life, and can go back there in the blink of an eye if I am not completely mindful.

I am not quite clear where this embellished sense of responsibility has come from but it seems to be a societal notion at this point for many. The days of questioning our worth have been replaced by how often the texts come in, how many e-mails overflow our inbox.

Do you remember the days when our phones were attached to a wall in the house? Oh, you were not born into that era? Okay, then I will explain: There was a time that the only phone we had was attached to the WALL! Yes, and not only that, but there was a time that the chord on the phone, which was attached to the wall, was so short that you couldn't even go into another room. On top of that, because most of us only had one phone, it needed to be centrally located, so it was normally in the kitchen. Yes, the kitchen! The one room in the house that was never empty was the room in which you were able to communicate with people other than your family. And then, god forbid, someone else was using the phone and you were optimistically waiting for a call, the person on the other end would simply get a busy signal, similar to the sound of a truck backing up. To make matters worse, you wouldn't even know that they had called.

That is right, there was a long period of time that voice mail did not even exist. I find myself getting anxious just thinking about it. I don't know how we survived. But somehow, here we are, acting like it is impossible.

I can remember the days when your family declared you were all going out, and you really wanted to stay in so you could sit by the phone. And you would go, because that was what you did, and then come home and have no idea if anyone had called you or not. Take that a bit farther in outrageousness—we sent our kids to college with these same phones. By the time I arrived at the University of Maryland, the chords on the phones were longer and you could actually slide into the hallway and pretend no one noticed.

It wasn't that bad, as a college student, but if you were the parent at home needing some attention, well, you just had to give that up. You were just going to have to call and call again, over and over. And even then, it was anyone's guess if you would get a call back.

To be honest, I can't remember ever hearing my mother say, "I've been trying to call you." As a matter of fact, I don't remember calling home that much either. We didn't have arguments about why I wasn't picking up or why I wasn't calling them back. I mean, I had classes to attend to, studying to be done, and friends to be had. You know, a whole life to live.

At what point did we give that up without a fight? At what point did we decide we could no longer make decisions without 'calling a friend'? At what point did we declare that life would be much better if we never had to make a decision alone again? And not just help with decision-making but help with everything!

Calling someone to sort out feelings, organize the day, help decide what you should eat, which house you should buy . . . At what point did we suddenly give up on the idea that we could pull off our day-to-day life as adults, all by ourselves?

I have the sense we might not have had that epiphany. That perhaps, instead, technology offered us more and more and more until this life in front of us became a life we could not live without. I'm not talking about the life inside of us; I am talking about the life in front of us. The one that continues to pull at our attention spans, keeping us from balance, peace, and happiness.

The sweet spot.

If we truly want the sweet spot of thinking like an organized person, we need to first take our power back. And in order to feel fully powerful, we need to do the unthinkable. We need to take a step back. And put the phone down . . . at least long enough to pause and create a space between ourselves and everything else.

That is the sweet spot.

4

PLANNING AS A WAY OF THINKING

The #1 reason people report that they don't sit down and make plans for the upcoming day is that they don't have time.

There is no time!

The claim is that each day continues to come at them with such force and intensity that the only shot they have of actually completing tasks is to quickly get into action as it comes.

In other words: Reacting.

A common challenge for humans is that all day long they move and jump, depending on what is coming their way. Their descriptions sound similar to the way my boys describe their Xbox games. Not to minimize the depths of what people are saying or experiencing, but the *response game* is just that. A game.

You can't see what is coming next, but you wait anxiously, with your trigger ready, to jump into action. Your body is poised, may even try to get a few tasks in while it waits, but then it comes, and no matter what was just happening, no matter what task was at hand, you respond to the next thing coming your way.

I once played the virtual reality video game with my son coaching me from the sidelines. I was nervous to have an audience, one I surely wanted to impress, but the fear was gone once the glasses were in place. Then I was actually inside this game.

"All you have to do is take your sword (which was really just a handle in my grip) and slice the pieces as they come at you. But do it fast, because if you don't, they will go right through you and you will lose points."

Sounded simple enough, though I knew better than to think any of these games are simple for me.

And so, I began chopping as quickly as I could. My right 'sword,' then left, then left again . . . ducking out of the way every once in a while since it seemed it was going to knock me down! My heart raced, but I stayed in it and kept at it. Mostly because I knew my kids were watching to see if I had any skills at all in this arena. I could tell I was doing pretty well and started to settle into a rhythm after a minute or two. I began to forget all about my audience watching me and was proud of myself for being able to pull off what seemed chaotic and out of my comfort zone.

As I finished and pulled off my VR goggles, I smiled proudly.

"I think I did pretty good!" I announced to my fifteen and eighteen-year-old who looked at me expressionless.

When I turned to look at my score, I was shocked. The game gave me a 60 percent score, which was clearly almost a failing grade. The kids were laughing. Not hysterically, but mostly because they thought it was funny that I was certain I was doing really well.

"It's pretty hard the first time," my eighteen-year-old assured me.

I was smart enough to understand that my eye-hand coordination has never been my strong suit and that I had zero experience at it, yet his empathy did not lesson my disappointment.

I was not disappointed in my losing score, though. The part that was actually disturbing was that while I was in it, slashing away at some pretend boulders flying at me, I was positive I was conquering them. I was certain I was winning! But I really wasn't. It was the mere illusion of the things I was able to hit, unaware of all that were apparently flying right by, that made me feel successful. Even when, in fact, I was a near failure at the game. Not to sound dramatic, but it's how I felt.

How does this relate to becoming an organized thinker?
It reminds me of how many clients share the management of their day.

Dan, twenty-eight years old, a software engineer and entrepreneur of a gaming company, arrived confidently to one of my workshops. He appeared well put together, confident, organized, with a pen in hand and a book to take notes in. He seemed focused, present, and serious and I wondered, with those three observations of him, how he needed me. Clearly he had left his desk in the middle of the afternoon to attend this brief workshop on organization, yet seemed to be able to compartmentalize so well that his attention surprised me.

When I mentioned what I noticed about him in just a few minutes of watching him, he laughed.

My experience had been that when professionals showed up focused and present, often they were almost where they needed to be organizationally speaking. His hint of laughter made me wonder if that were true.

"How do you keep track of everything that you need to, given that you run a company of your own and then help manage another one? That must be a lot of work!"

"Yea, things are coming at me all day long," he replied calmly.

"Do you currently have a system for keeping track of the tasks that need to be completed?"

"Well, I have a really good memory," he said, "So I keep the running list in my head."

I suddenly knew why he had arrived at this workshop.

It was like my gaming experience. While in the thick of it, I had the sense I was successful, effective, and efficient, yet once I stepped out of it, I could see that I was not quite as successful as I had thought.

With youth on his side, as well as confidence, he believed he could retain the details he needed to complete tasks at hand in an efficient and effective manner. I mean, if you are quick to jump from one task to another, isn't that the epitome of effectiveness?

Rarely ever.

The truth was that he had become so accustomed to reacting at a minute's notice that he wasn't able to access the thought process of an organized person at all. Instead, he was left to working long hours, feeling exasperated as each day ended with tasks not completed.

Feeling challenged and frustrated by a lack of focus and a constant state of being overwhelmed (with a new baby on the way!), he became slightly open to the fact that there might be a better and more efficient way.

Sometimes, all we can do is just show up and see what is available.

Planning is not another thing to do

We need to think of planning as a thought process rather than another thing to do. We already have too much to do!

This basic principle is why people do not take the time to plan. Clearly Dan's plate was already overloaded, so the idea of taking additional time to write all that was on his mind seemed like a pure waste of time. Add that to the fact he was convinced his memory was beyond capable of retaining all these tasks. So, what would be the point?

Here is the problem with counting on your memory. While you are working on tasks, your brain is doing its best to recall the other things left on the list. It knows that you are counting on it for later, so it keeps at it all day long. Imagine that? Asking part of your brain to work on the task in front of you while asking the other part of your brain to hold onto what has to be done next. And not just the very next task, but all the tasks?!

Can you pat your head and rub your stomach in circles at the same time?

Okay, maybe you can, but you get the point!

That's a lot to ask of your brain, especially with an expectation of completing the work with complete satisfaction.

Here is where the *thinking* part comes in. The organized thinking person, who is able to keep stress levels low and productivity high, does not look at organizing this list as another job. Instead, they look at the list as something that needs to be mentally organized in order to begin working in a clear-headed way.

Compartmentalizing your thoughts.

And yes, in order to compartmentalize your thoughts so that you can think and produce like an organized thinker, you will need to *write it down*.

The critical part is to not get fearful or overwhelmed that you now have to think of yourself as an organized person. That could be an entire life change for many people. That could also be the one that causes feelings of being overwhelmed, as well as resistance, which will only worsen your current state of mind.

As confident as Dan was the day he told me about his ability to remember, he willingly took on this way of thinking like an organized person and began to write out his tasks at the end of each day, in preparation for the next day.

After several weeks, and relentless fine-tuning, he began to see the shift in his focus.

"I do feel the value in being able to physically see on paper what I need to get done. Instead of having to do mental games to figure out what and when everything needs to get done, I can simply jot it down. It seems like a simple thing, but just being able to see it allows me to have longer periods of focus. And with this job, I need that to be successful."

5

INVESTING IN THE PLAN, NOT THE OUTCOME

I was excited as I began my Monday morning ritual of heading to the coffee shop to follow through with my self-imposed writing goals. I felt organized and successful, knowing that no one cared about my task at hand, and no one would be let down if I didn't do it. I felt empowered that I was leaving normal home-office routines behind, in hopes of being more productive. I wasn't on a mission exactly, just an understanding that when I changed my atmosphere, I created new, unforeseen possibilities and a greater chance of honoring my word. It wasn't difficult to leave my comfy and quiet home office; I just needed to declare I was going to do it.

Sometimes, that declaration is challenging. But not on this day.

I had changed out of my usual workout gear, thrown on what I considered a work outfit—fancy jeans, T-shirt, and high-heeled sandals—and found the perfect spot with my overpriced coffee drink. I felt giddy about having two and a half hours of meticulously planned out writing time. I felt proud of my ability to plan time alone, time to be productive and time to get s**t done. I felt smitten about my planning, to be honest.

As I detailed my planner and all that I needed to get done today, as well as what I needed to get done this week, I sat back in my chair with my fingertips perched and ready to write.

Planning! All we need to conquer success is some real planning.

Out of the corner of my eye, I watched a woman settle into her space in front of me. I held my fingers in place and thought, aha, another woman with real intention. While she was still in her workout gear, I could see that it was simply her comfort work gear as she began to set up the work equipment she needed to begin working. I could see the intention not just in her eyes, but in everything she did. Mostly, I was obsessed with her cleaning ritual! Being a neat freak myself, I watched in awe and wondered if I needed to add some more rituals to my 'work' situation at Starbucks.

She pulled out a wet wipe from her bag and proceeded to wipe everything down. Everything. She carefully wiped the entire outside of her laptop, lifting it so she could wipe the underside of it as well. She then reached over and carefully cleaned the cover of her phone, lifting it also, and cleaning all angles of her iPhone. But she wasn't done there. She then wiped down the whole table, again lifting everything so she could get under each thing she had just placed on the table.

I wondered what kind of business she was working on and applauded her ability to be so focused on creating the perfect spot for her work. I also wondered where I could get those wipes and if I should be wiping down my equipment too!

I was even relieved that she was directly in front of me, since I had often been distracted by people not as serious about working as I was. I did not need any talkers distracting me today.

My plan was to begin writing as soon as she was settled and ready to start as well. Little did she know that we were about to share this workspace and were going to spend the morning working together. She had become my accountability partner without knowing it.

It seemed like she was almost done, when she carefully lifted her grand, frothy Starbucks drink and began to use the same wet wipe to wipe down every inch of the cup. She then moved it a bit closer to her things, tidying everything up just so, then walked to the garbage to throw the wipe out.

I was perched and ready to start working.

She sat back in her seat, moving her laptop about an inch forward to get it in just the right spot, and I knew for sure it was time. Except, in that moment, she misjudged just ONE thing.

As her laptop slid back, she hit the cup (the one she had just cleaned) ever so slightly, knocking the whole thing onto its side! Ice, drink, and all . . . spilling all over the tiny table, falling onto the chair on the other side of the table. The chair that held her backpack—that she had just spent the past five minutes carefully pulling all of her important things out of.

She sat motionless for what seemed like the longest ten seconds of my life, no doubt in shock, as my heart raced right along with hers.

All of that work. Meticulously planning her morning, her things, the care needed to clean all of her devices, her great intention to have a successful morning and successful day. And now, everything was a mess!

Would she leave? Would she go home? Would she flip out? I felt panicked.

But she did not appear ruffled at all.

Instead, she walked calmly to the same place she had just thrown away her wet wipe and now grabbed a handful of napkins. I wanted her to run back to the table to start cleaning before it reached her laptop, but she didn't. She just walked, shaking her head a bit with each step. She then proceeded to stop the flow of coffee with her wad of paper towels, piled the heap of napkins on the table, then went to the cashier, and told her about the spill.

That was what she did. My hands still perched on my laptop, heart racing, and ready to call it a day, I watched in awe. She was so calm that I wondered if this had happened to her before.

The cashier then helped her diligently to clean up the mess, even mopping up the floor, and within five minutes, it was all cleaned up, complete with a freshly-filled coffee drink set up on the table.

And that was that. She settled back into her chair and began to work as if nothing had ever happened. And so did I.

The sweet spot of the story was that we were both prepared. We had a plan, intention, and the right mindset for a successful day. As a matter of fact, I would say that it was only due to the plans that we made independently that helped both of us stay focused on our original goal. Not letting a near disaster get in the way.

Because that is the thing about plans. All we can do is make them. And then hope that the universe moves in sync with them as we hope. Sometimes it will and sometimes it won't, but we can be sure that we have a much better chance of the success we hope for when we at least begin with a plan.

6

ORGANIZATION AND STRUCTURE = SUCCESS

Do you often wonder why it is so challenging to follow through with the thoughts in your mind? Why, even when you write them out as clearly as you can, they don't manifest in the way you are thinking? You are intelligent, educated, confident, and have so many great ideas, so why doesn't it come out just the way you have it figured out in your mind?

It actually isn't that complicated and is very common. The fact is that your passion and a head filled with ideas is not enough on its own. While it helped to give you the courage to begin in the first place, it will not be enough to sustain efficiency and effectiveness on a daily basis, no matter how much you love what you do. As a matter of fact, the longer you try to ride on the fumes of your enthusiasm, the longer it will take you to create true financial success.

First, the ideas you have flowing through your mind day in and day out are a meaningful start but will not create movement on their own. In fact, pretty quickly they will begin to hinder your progress. If you have been thinking about the same or even new ideas for weeks or months, grab a notebook now so you can write them out and organize them.

Rather than creating a list, though, give each page in your notebook a different topic.

Here are some examples:

- Expenses
- Profit
- Time
- Marketing
- Daily routines
- Weekly, monthly, yearly goals.

Once you have done that, you will already begin to see the larger picture, but it is just the beginning. Next, you will need to be as detailed as you can on each topic as you add timelines and deadlines. This is the sweet spot in creating financial success.

True success will come when you spend more time on tasks creating money, rather than writing lists, creating ideas, and thinking about what you want to do next. True success will come when you are able to design clear details about your daily routines and how each one of them will make money. True success will come when you know what each day will look like, and have clear details of how the work today will meet the goals you've set for the month and year as well. Each task needs to be connected to the bigger goal, which needs to be connected to your financial bottom line.

Once you are organized in your thoughts and have designed the structure of the work you do, you will be able to get into action. If you feel yourself perseverating on the end goal and doing more thinking than doing, visualize your job as an actual building. Notice how an actual building has the base being the largest part of the structure to create stability. It wouldn't work any other way, right? I mean, if you flipped your building or business upside down, with the largest part at the top, eventually your building would topple over! In the same way, if you fill your days with grand ideas about the future of your business or career without the base to stabilize it, everything will topple over as well.

Design real organization and structure and get busy in the doing part! That is what will lead you to success.

7

SECURE THE BASE NOW; SECURE YOUR WEALTH LATER

Consider yourself the builder with capabilities of creating tremendous buildings, castles, even whole communities . . . you have the ability, the power, and the knowledge. Imagine now, you hastily hand off to your $8/hour workers the job of building the base—the base of the building, the castle, even the gigantic community—as you run about your day getting pieces to continue to build with. When you return, you see clearly that the base is not done well. There are pieces missing, and the pieces that are completed are not done well.

What do you do now? You have three choices:

- Hope it is strong enough to hold what you are about to create on top, always wondering how long it can hold.
- Get rid of all of your people, tear it down, and start over, leaving yourself exhausted, but left to build the rest.
- Begin taking the base apart with the help of your team, and then begin helping them to rebuild it in the solid design you know it needs.

Whether you are a business owner, entrepreneur or manager, it's important to remember that everything should be connected to each piece of the business. There should be one theme, main idea, and sole purpose of the business that resonates in everyone and everything involved in the business.

Everything should be taken into account and nothing taken for granted when it comes to your success. Nothing is too large to be completely redone and nothing too small to be overlooked. The challenging part is remaining patient with the whole process, willing to focus on each aspect of the business, one part at a time, with realistic timelines of when each should be operating efficiently and to its best ability. All structures need a structurally sound base; without that, any one particular storm could force you to close the doors.

Stay committed to your original goal of being a successful business for years to come. Here are the basics of what you need to consider:

The administrative team:
1 – Administrative leaders who have clearly-defined systems for all their employees.
2 – Directors and managers who create weekly, monthly, and yearly accountability for their team.

The frontline:
1 – Personable, helpful, and knowledgeable staff that creates a welcoming first impression of your business.
2 – Well-trained staff that understands their role in selling the company.

The plan:
1 – Daily systems that are reliable, plant seeds for the future, and create new business.
2 – Business plans that include yearly financial growth goals.
3 – Marketing plans that involve small- and large-scale advertising that is consistent, yet always evolving to meet the needs of the economy.

Securing the base of your business now will secure your financial wealth later.

8

MESS CAUSES STRESS

Whether you prefer a messy desk or simply say that because you can't seem to get it to be any other way, you are suffering from the consequences of it.

Mess causes stress.

A twenty-one-year-old college student suffering from severe panic attacks said it best.

"Daily things like staying in bed all day and feeling constantly anxious about the mess (of my room) I was living in now don't even come up because I have a plan each day and don't let it get to that point."

After just three months of working together, she developed a new voice that reminded her of what to do, before panic about the impending panic attacks occurred. She still doesn't consider herself an organized person, but she thinks like one and has a plan of attack in advance, which helps her reap the benefits of producing like an organized person.

I asked her if she was aware of the mess before and the possibility that it caused her some anxiety, and she said that she knew she didn't like it, but also that she didn't have time to fix it as often as it needed it, so she would ignore it.

The organized mind knows that we cannot ignore things simply because we say we are going to. Often, the more we try to ignore it, the more it distracts us.

Another emerging adult I worked with would say that the mess on the floor of all his clothes was comforting because he could see what he had and didn't have to look for it. That was what he *said*.

We all justify the things we do. This justification gives us the permission to hold onto habits that don't serve us well. Like cleaning up.

It wasn't until much later that he admitted his truth. "I actually prefer it cleaned up. It's just that I don't like taking the time to do it. When it is clean and everything is in its place, I can actually think better."

Again, it always comes back to thinking!

A thirty-year-old data input professional described *needing* to clean his room, but refused to believe why he needed to do it since he lived alone.

"What do you feel when you walk into your room and see the mess?" I asked.

"I feel like a failure," he said, without missing a beat.

Enough said. "There is your why!"

How can we expect to feel successful in our jobs, lives, and relationships when the simple act of not cleaning up our living spaces makes us feel like a failure?

Clearly you are not a failure because of a messy room, but that is not the point. The point is that it all comes back to how you think. Not just about things in their place, but the commentary you have about yourself due to the things not being in their place.

9

THE EASY STUFF. THAT'S ALWAYS THE HARDEST TO FIND

Do you know people in your life, maybe even that you live with, that always know where everything is? That person. *The finder in your group.* The one that everyone turns to when something can't be found. Do you wonder how it's possible for one person to keep track of all of their own things while still having an idea of where other people's things are?

Finding things in real life is very similar to the card game we all played at a young age: *The Memory Game.*

I like that the name of the game doesn't try to cover up the skills necessary to play the game well. We used to set the cards up in even rows and columns, all face down. Then each person would take their turn flipping one card over, and the other one secretly over, to see if it matched. The other player would not get to see the second card, but always the first. Of course, if it was a match, you got to take the pair! And go again.

That makes sense. There is always a reward in being able to find what you are looking for! In the beginning, the game appears more like a research project in search of clues, with each person quickly choosing one, then two cards, and placing them right back down. The only way to find a match at first is just plain good luck. Yet, as the game continues, and at least half have been revealed, the first one to not treat the game like a random lottery ticket will end up winning.

The *Finder* in your life never treated this childhood game as a lottery ticket. Your finder, instead, had a secret but methodical plan. Each time the finder chose a card, a thought process arose, and a few questions were asked silently.

Have I seen that card before?

If yes, *where did I see that card?*

And then a command, *let's remember where this one is.*

But even that last command needed more detail by noting, *it is two down and one away from the right.*

The same questions follow for the second card—each time trying to recall where or if it had been seen and trying to create a memory for the new one seen.

Why am I carrying on about this childhood game you never really cared for?

Simple. This is the memory game of your life. This is the thinking of the organized person you know.

The *finder.*

It is not pure luck.

Have you ever heard them say, "If you would put your keys on the key rack, you wouldn't lose them!" Well, obviously. Cue laughter.

But for the organized person, they know what the sweet spot is, and it is not having an amazing memory.

I am the perfect example. I do not have a great memory. As a matter of fact, in college, when I would read new and difficult material, I would often need to reread it, then highlight, and sometimes rewrite what I had highlighted, before I felt confident enough to remember it. Yet, I AM the finder in the house!

And people that know me do refer to me as being organized. I am.

I began to think like an organized person the first day I realized I could not always rely on my memory. The first tool I established was the power of writing. I was well aware that if I wrote it down, I did not have to rely on my memory, and could then still recall the information I needed to recall. Or, find the things I needed to find.

In addition to writing things down to recall important topics, though, I began to play the memory card game with my things.

I have always hated wasting time. The idea of spending several hours or days searching for things drives me crazy. It kept me from doing important things that needed to get done and would put my mind into overtime, unable to let go of the search even when I wasn't looking for it.

I would be driving my car to work and thinking: *What jacket was I wearing when I saw it last?*

I would be having dinner with friends and thinking: *When was the last time I remember holding that in my hand?*

My mental search for it would become obsessive with barely any way to turn it off, until I bought a new one or found it. Often, I would buy a new one and then find it, which would infuriate me because I hated to waste money, almost as much as wasting my time.

In comes the purpose of the Memory Card Game.

Two down and one from the right. Got it!

The memory game of life

Let's start with the morning ritual: Time to leave for work.

Is it time to leave for work? Or was it time to leave for work twenty minutes ago? As you arrive at the door, you realize you don't have your keys.

Lost keys can make a mess of an entire day, even if they are only misplaced momentarily. More than the time lost searching for them, the stress we endure while searching, with the impending doom of all that will or may happen if we don't find them, is now how you begin the day. Under duress.

The organized thinker is mindful of the thoughts needed to have a successful day.

When it is time to go, it is time to go.

So why don't we pay better attention to what we do with our keys?

Well, most likely we don't think about it, because we are too busy worrying about everything else. And because, well, this key hanging thing is so small on the scale of all the other things we are trying to manage, it doesn't even grab our attention.

We don't pay attention to the details of having a specific spot for our keys because we don't think like an organized person.

Let's see if this is true for you.

You are just getting home from a long day at the office followed by a well-needed run to the gym. You park your car in the lot, have your briefcase on one shoulder, your gym bag on the other, and the half-empty water bottle in your hand. You drop your keys in the side of the gym bag so you can open the door and drop your bags at the front door as you enter. The water bottle makes it to the kitchen counter and the gym bag makes it up the stairs to your room.

You head back down the stairs and are starving, but still need to take the dog out. By the time you get back in again, all you can think about is eating and sitting down to relax and watch some TV. Later that night, you head upstairs, see your gym bag on the floor, and remember to pull the wet clothes out of it before putting the bag into your closet.

And you already know what happens tomorrow as you are getting ready to leave for work—no keys and no idea where they are.

Here is where two down and one to the right comes in handy!

The organized thinker strategically places things in their rightful spot because they are aware that one moment of pause now could save hours of searching later.

If we look at this same example again, the thought process might look like this:

> *Upon getting out of the car and gathering all of my things, half-starved, I note items of importance: keys, wallet, glasses. As I get to the door, I see that something has to shift, but I think in terms of matches.*

What goes with what? Stay with me here, even though I know you are already thinking that this is too much thinking for something simple like a set of keys. You're wondering: *Why can't I just put them down?*

You can. But if you want more time in your life to enjoy things other than *searching* hang in there.

Matches.

As I get to the door, I know that if I put the water bottle in my gym bag, at least it makes sense. They go together. So even if I am panicked later that I can't find my water bottle, I can refer to my memory match game and will no doubt remember—gym bag!

Another solution would be to put the keys in a pocket, but not a pocket that doesn't have anything to do with starting the car or going to work. It has to make sense in terms of when you will need them again. If I put them in my coat pocket, chances are likely that I will put that same coat on the next time I am leaving the house, and there they will be!

But that doesn't work for me because I rarely wear the same jacket two days in a row. However, if I stick the keys in my back pocket, which clearly don't fit in there, but can hold them for a minute, I will be forced to take them out on getting into the house, because they are uncomfortable and quietly calling to be taken out!

That's actually the best scenario, because if I am forced to take them out as soon as I walk in the door, I will then also remember to put them on the key rack that I have by each exit of the house. Not only that, but as I am putting my keys there, I will also be reminded that that is where my wallet needs to go too because it also matches. Both items will be needed the next time I leave the house.

For the small but necessary things in life, we need to be mindful at all times of matches, as well as being prepared with a specific place holder, which will also become an automatic match!

10

LIFE-CHANGING MORNING RITUALS

It's safe to say that human beings spend more time complaining about life experiences than finding joy in them, or fixing the ones that cause despair.

It is everywhere! It's at the water cooler, the staff lounge, the gym, the coffee shop... I actually can't think of one place where a group of people convene in their daily life that is a complaint-free zone. And guess what? The more we complain about what we do not want, the more the problem persists, so we stay frozen in this pattern that often begins the moment we awake in the morning.

You don't complain in the morning when you wake up?

Okay... then what was that voice that yelled at you when the alarm went off this morning that convinced you to hit the snooze for seven more minutes of sleep? The voice that convinced you seven minutes was going to be just what you needed? What did that voice say?

How can it be morning already? I'm too tired. I'll go to the gym a different time. I will skip a shower. I hate the cold. I need more sleep...

Whatever your voice says, I'll bet it does not live in a space of gratitude, and that this small act (hitting the snooze button) that you repeat almost every morning is how you design many of your days.

Life by design
Organization in your life begins the moment you open your eyes. That's the good news, because at any moment, you can decide to change the ritual that has now become a habit.

Change your mind, change your life
Morning rituals will change your mind, your day, and your life. This has been researched and proven over and over again. And, quite honestly, just makes sense. In order to have the life we want, we must be able to create an intention about everything in our life. Pretending that setting an alarm is intention enough is like expecting the coffee pot to make coffee before adding water. The coffee is not coming!

Setting morning rituals that create a positive start will trickle down into the rest of the day. The rituals do not have to be complicated. They don't even have to involve a workout, if that's not what you are up to right now.

> The action part: Creating rituals in advance.
> The thought process: Designing, not reacting to our life at hand.

Here are some simple suggestions:
1 – Creating intention
Action: Declare how many hours of sleep you need and plan your bedtime around that declaration.

Mindset: I need eight hours of sleep to feel focused and am committed to being more focused.

2 – Alarms
Action: Set the alarm, adjusting your nighttime schedule so you can honor your sleep commitment. Put your alarm (clock, phone) far enough away that you must get out of bed to reach it.

Mindset: I am creating a morning that I am excited about, so I am not going to hit the snooze and miss out on it.

3 – Reset
Action: Declare what you will do in the morning that will entice you to get up! Examples—watching a favorite morning show, meditation (The Headspace app is great!), exercise, long, brisk walk with the dog, listening to music, sitting by the fireplace with a cup of coffee.

Mindset: I am going to be tired when the alarm goes off, but I know I have slept enough and am looking forward to starting the day with something that makes me feel good. Rushing around does not make me feel good.

4 – Preparation
Action: The night before you are ready to reset, make sure everything is in its place to help you be successful. If you are planning on waking at 6 a.m. and want to do fifteen minutes of yoga, have your mat laid out, a candle close by, and even a water bottle ready to go. If you want to sit by the fire and have coffee, set up the coffee machine the night before, have music close by, and a journal or a book too, so you have options.

Mindset: A few extra minutes at night will guarantee I get what I need in the morning without much thought.

5 – Ritual
Action: Hear the alarm and open your eyes. Set your phone to a song you like and then allow yourself to listen to the whole song with your eyes closed (no sleeping!). This will set the stage for what is next . . . turning it off so you can get to your morning.

Mindset: Perfect . . . another day to live a life that I have designed! It is my life and I am in charge of it.

Your morning ritual could be fifteen minutes or an hour. Get what you need! If it means going to bed a few minutes earlier so you can wake up earlier to get it, then do it. This is your life. No one is going to hand you a bag of happiness. Only *you* can create it.

My morning ritual is simple but just what I need—coffee in hand, my daily reflection book, my dog at my feet, and the fire warming me up for another great day. And when the alarm goes off, I know that all I have to do to set this day on the right path is to wake up and go downstairs.

11

WORK FROM HOME ORGANIZATION

The point of planning isn't to know exactly what to do. The point of planning is to delude yourself into thinking you know what you're doing just long enough for you to actually get off your ass and start.

—*Mark Manson*

Finally, your dream has come true! The job that allows you to work from home. All of that long-awaited freedom to design your own schedule. The ability to create your day based on what is best for you. Finding the times of day when you are most productive, making sure you are able to fit in your workouts, picking up the kids, prescriptions, doctor appointments . . . all from the comfort of your own home.

Finally, a life by design.

Freedom

And so the first day begins. Blissfully. You wake up early naturally with excitement. I mean, the day is all yours. You have a full day of to-do items but you are so excited about being able to do it your way that your adrenalin is on overdrive.

First . . . self-care. You grab a small breakfast, throw on your running shoes, and decide to gift yourself a short run to get the juices flowing. Why not? You have ALLLLL day.

But while you are out, you feel so great, that you decide to lean in and keep going. Why stop at three miles when you feel this good? So, you make an executive decision to run until you begin to feel tired and, lo and behold, you end up running an hour. You can hear silent cheers in the background of your mind.

This is so great. I'm running for an hour and still have the whole day ahead to get my work done. I just knew this was going to be amazing!

You get back home, get showered and dressed, feeling tickled that you can throw on a pair of jeans with your favorite sweatshirt, and head back to the kitchen for a light snack. It's almost hard to imagine how excited you could feel about getting to work.

Just as you sit at your desk and open your computer, you feel slightly overwhelmed by the amount of e-mails sitting in your inbox. So you take a deep breath and know just what you need. Coffee!

Clearly aware that you shouldn't leave the house again, you brew a simple cup of coffee yourself, add the fix-ins, and head back to your desk. One sip of coffee and you begin to run through all of the things you need to do today. Then head back into your inbox to start checking off the e-mails.

As you go through the work e-mails, you take the time needed to respond to each and open the junk ones, just to see if it is something you should save or send to trash. As you open the unnecessary ones, you begin to get sidetracked by the details.

There is a sale at Kohls, plus the coupon they just sent, which makes you scroll your memory bank for the things you had put on a list that are needed for the party next week . . .

You take a minute to pause as your cell phone begins to sound, which is when you notice it is noon!

Suddenly, this WHOLE day you had has turned into three more hours until the kids come home from school and that is only if you skip lunch.

Now your heart is racing in a whole different way. Panic.

Here is the truth about the freedom of working from home. Unless you are organized or at least willing to create a system for yourself, and are able to hold yourself accountable, the freedom can quickly become a curse. Whether you are the kind of person that loses track of time easily and can't get work done, or are the one who can hyper focus on work and then loses track of the world around you, you should commit to a system.

The sweet spot to becoming an organized thinker is in finding balance. That's it.

The good news is that even if having a daily organization system is not your natural inclination, it is easy enough to design one that works for you and fits into your daily life. All you need to do is create it and have an intention to follow through with it.

Having a morning routine is a great place to start, even if it means that on different days you have different rituals. Maybe some mornings you wake up and head to the gym, while other mornings you begin working as soon as you are up and showered for the day. The beauty is that *you* get to decide.

The real balance comes in designing a schedule that allows you to fit in the things that must be done, rolling in the ones that should be done, and then making time for the ones you want to get done.

Planning is critical:
It is critical that you begin planning the night before. Do not wait until Monday morning to sit down and decide how your day and week will work. Monday will set a tone for the week and should be mapped out in advance so that it is your most productive day. After all, you have had two days prior to that to get some R&R, so let's not slide that into day three.

Choosing a calendar:
I know many of us are glued to our iPhones and google calendars, which I agree are very helpful! Unfortunately, if this is your only tool, it becomes challenging to account for all that has to be completed.

The most helpful form of calendar I have used and that I recommend is one that allows you to see one month at a glance as well as one week at a glance, so you can write in upcoming appointments and commitments,. If you can find one you like that also allows you to add simple to-do lists within the week at a glance, you will find it easy to hold yourself accountable.

And since you no longer have a boss checking over your shoulder, you will be responsible for your own accountability.

Planning the week:
Sunday is a great time to take twenty to thirty minutes to simply look at the week ahead. Add all the appointments that you have for the week as well as reminders. Once you have added in the actual appointments, add in things that you know you want to do. Things that might not necessarily be work items, but perhaps things that help you focus during the day. Maybe you enjoy reading, meditating, or going for a run. Maybe you find you are most focused after your workout or right before, knowing you will be treating yourself to a workout.

You get to decide. But do it with intention.

Next, create blocks of time to get specific tasks done. For instance, if you have a work project due on Friday, calculate how long you think it will take to complete it, then declare how much time you can spend in one sitting. This is important. If you know this is a project that will take six hours, and know that it is a challenging one, or that you can only sit still for two hours, then don't add a six-hour block to your schedule on Thursday.

The goal is to create a schedule that you can tackle with success. So be realistic as to your strengths and weaknesses, rather than scheduling the way you think you should be able to handle it.

If you know that two hours in one sitting can be accomplished easily, great! Schedule three different two-hour blocks—perhaps on Monday, Tuesday, and Wednesday. This leaves room for error. Maybe you will surprise yourself and, by Tuesday, be completely done. Perfect. Yet if the opposite happens, and by Wednesday you still need more time, you can add another block to Thursday.

Get it?

Design it with realistic balance and intuition that will entice accountability.

Plan for changes:
This is not like that diet you keep starting and stopping. If you are able to do this with intention, it will not only work, but you will be able to sleep better and be more productive all week long. However, it is important to remember that life will happen and there will no doubt be a call from the school nurse, a flat tire, an unexpected trip to the doctor . . . but if you are prepared for what to do next, you can still be successful.

When life occurs on its terms, first lower your shoulders and take a look at what you had planned for the day. Is there someone you need to call to reschedule? What can you move from today's plans to another day this week? Do not make the mistake of simply sliding everything from today to tomorrow. While that might seem like a great idea in theory, it merely creates a schedule by convenience, not by intention. Before anything in the schedule is moved, carefully note what is already scheduled for that next day and then strategically place today's items in appropriate dates where it can be completed.

12

ORGANIZING MAIL

This may seem like a topic that doesn't deserve a whole chapter by itself. That it isn't that important or that it might not need as much attention. Yet what I have seen is that while this is a small topic, the ramifications of not giving proper attention to mail or not being mindful of the importance of the mail can result in some negative consequences.

Think about it. It's the mail

While managing the mail has become easier with online billing, in a way, having bills come across the computer screen, rather than in the mailbox, has somehow added to our difficulty in managing simple tasks like *the mail*.

The organized thinker knows that time wasted looking for a missing bill, or making several calls to get the late fee waived, is not a good use of time and is not the path to efficiency, effectiveness, or productivity. Actually, you probably know that as well, but have trouble avoiding it.

However, you don't have to be organized to create a simple home/office mail system, and once you complete it, you merely follow through with your plan.

To design a system that is safe, reliable, and productive you will need *mail spot*. One designated area that is just for mail, nothing else. If you can create this simple process of creating a place for mail, you will eliminate many other things in your life that cause chaos and sometimes stress as well.

Are you rolling your eyes? If you are, then you might also be unaware of all the other things that occur in your life that feel chaotic, simply because you don't have a system around organizing your mail.

Let's take a normal day. You are on the way home from work, have picked up the kids from school, and have dinner on your mind, with no thought about what you are going to make, but your mind is still trying to sort out the day. As you roll into the driveway, one child is talking about how hungry he is. The other is crying due to his exhaustion. You all get out of the car and remember to grab the mail from the mailbox.

As you get into the house, you drop your briefcase carefully near your desk, you drop your keys on the kitchen counter, and add the mail to the ever-growing pile sitting beside the microwave. A thought occurs to you to look through the mail, but at that same moment, the child that was once crying in the car now seems to be doubled over in pain on the couch.

Just another long weekday . . .

That slight moment of interruption is never just one day, but a continuation of all of the days from before. How many days go by before you have a moment to breathe and actually look at that pile stacked neatly (or not so neatly) near the microwave?

Don't think there are any ramifications from not looking at the mail for a few days? Here are just a few that you may not have considered:

- Not knowing where things are clutters other parts of your day as you search for missing items.
- Bills often don't get paid on time.
- Late notices become very late notices.
- Deadlines are missed.
- Extra money and time is spent.

Eliminating any one of these things will instantly create space and time in your mind and in your life and help you become more focused on daily tasks at hand.

13

ORGANIZING OUR THOUGHTS THROUGH BREATHING

It's hard to believe, but much of what we feel resonates in our breathing.

Think about the last time you felt anxious or stressed about something. Anything. There are plenty of examples—interview day, race day, traveling, presenting, etc.

Now try to recall how you feel physically during those moments. Perhaps your heart races. Or your adrenalin rushes so furiously that you can feel your heart beat in your ears. Can you actually hear the pounding?

How do you feel emotionally while this is happening?

Perhaps you feel as though you are going to get physically sick, or maybe that you need to lie down. Maybe you feel paralyzed with fear? No matter what you feel at that time, each physical sensation feeds into your emotional well-being and vice versa.

They basically work together to create one giant sense of being overwhelmed and in a minute's notice, you can switch from being nervous to being completely unable to think clearly at all.

Perhaps you fear you won't remember anything that you practiced the night before or that your legs won't be able to compete in the race or that you simply will stumble on all of your words in an interview that you were clearly once prepared for.

The organized thinker even compartmentalizes his/her own breathing.

If we can merely learn to alter or control our breathing, we will not only relieve the physical sensations, but the emotional sensations associated as well.

Surely you have heard the quote: "Mind over matter. If you don't mind, it doesn't matter." How true that is! And the best part of that is that even if it does matter, we can convince ourselves that in this moment we don't mind . . . just by becoming more mindful about our breathing.

Box breathing

Box breathing, also known as square breathing, is a technique used when taking slow, deep breaths. It can heighten performance and concentration while also being a powerful stress reliever. Some also refer to it is four-square breathing.

It is a great technique that will help reduce stress and anxiety and can be used under any circumstances. Athletes, Navy Seals, police officers, and nurses are well versed in this technique. However, anyone can use it and will find relief. As a matter of fact, according to the Mayo Clinic, there's evidence that intentional deep breathing can actually calm and regulate the autonomic nervous system. This process can lower blood pressure and provide an almost immediate sense of calm.

Getting started

Before you get started, make sure you are seated in an upright position with your feet flat on the floor. It is helpful if you can be in a stress-free, quiet environment, especially while beginning this practice, so that you can focus deeply on your breathing.

Keep your hands relaxed in your lap with your palms facing up and focus on your posture. In order to achieve deep breathing, you should be sitting up straight.

Slowly exhale

While sitting upright, slowly exhale through your mouth. The goal is to release all of the oxygen from your lungs. Do this slowly and with great intention, doing your best to keep all other thoughts out of your mind.

Slowly inhale
Then inhale slowly and deeply through your nose to the count of four. In this step, count to four very slowly in your head. Imagine that you can feel the air filling your lungs, one section at a time, until your lungs are completely full and the air is able to move into your abdomen.

Hold your breath
Now hold your breath for another slow count of four.

Exhale again
Exhale through your mouth for the same slow count of four, expelling the air from your lungs and abdomen. Become acutely aware of the air leaving your lungs.

Hold your breath again
This time, hold your breath for the same slow count of four and then repeat this whole process.

This process produces a calm and relaxed feeling in the mind and body and can reduce stress and improve your mood. It can also help treat insomnia by allowing you to calm your nervous system at night before going to bed, as well as managing pain and erratic moods during the day.

Additionally, once you have mastered Box Breathing, you will see that it can be helpful in any situation that suddenly triggers an emotion that keeps you from being productive, thoughtful, and happy.

14

THE CALENDAR

The organized thinker knows that when you attempt to keep all tasks in the memory bank, each task is secretly disrupted by the tasks your mind is trying to hold onto. That is why the organized thinker writes everything down.

Client: Technical Engineer, Entrepreneur, CEO of a Gaming Company, thirty years old.

"How do you keep track of all that you need to do?" This is my usual, starting question for any client that feels like their focus is lacking, and/or they are not as efficient as they could be during any given day.

"That's easy. I have a very good memory," he said.

I looked to see if he was going to laugh, but it clearly wasn't a joke.

"So, you keep a mental log of everything you have to do?"

"Yes."

I did not question his memory or ability to retain large amounts of data. After all, he is a successful engineer. However, I know for sure that one of the most common reasons successful business people have difficulty staying on task and being efficient is their lack of an organized system. A system that provides clear boundaries—compartmentalizing what has to be done, how long it will take, and when it needs to be completed.

By forcing yourself to memorize what has to be done, your mind works overtime all day long.

This scenario reminded me of a time about a decade ago when I was doing my best to understand how the iPhone worked. I remember complaining to my son, who was studying engineering at the time.

"This phone constantly needs to be charged," I said. "The battery never even lasts a full day."

"That's because you probably don't close your apps," he said matter-of-factly.

I thought that was ridiculous. I mean, clearly I would open an app, finish using it, then go to the next one. Anyone could see that the first one had closed.

Or hadn't it?

Perspective is everything. And just because we can't see that something is creating interference, it does not mean that it isn't causing interference.

"Of course, I close my apps," I said, like a mother in charge of her life.

"Okay then, let me see your phone."

And at that, he pushed the middle button twice and there, before my eyes, were many boxes. Many! Hmmmm.

"What you have to do is slide each one of them out of the screen. Then, they are actually closed. But until then, what you have is a battery working overtime with all of your apps open, even when you aren't currently working in those apps."

This was shocking to me. The fact that my battery was continuing to work overtime on apps that I couldn't even see anymore, and the fact that no one had mentioned that I should be closing them one at a time.

Maybe as you read this, you feel it is obvious. However, I'm pretty sure that the very first time you were told that, you had many apps open as well!

This is remotely what is happening in your mind. Without a system in place, ideas come into your mind in the morning and you begin to play games with the lists, moving each task around in your mind from space to space, figuring out when and where these will fit into your day and week.

Then the phone rings and three more tasks are added. Ten more e-mails come in and several more tasks are added. A co-worker calls needing help with a project and more tasks are added.

Yet, because you have a great memory, you keep storing each task into the dark space of your brain and are certain you will recall them as needed. Which is when you sit at your desk, coffee in hand, and begin your work. Surprisingly, even though you are certain you have a hundred things to do, you are not sure where to start. You open your e-mail one more time to see if you can trigger your memory on something that needs attention first and easily find it.

And so, you begin!

Although in those first few minutes you may feel efficient and effective, your memory bank is working overtime trying to hold onto all of those other things that need to be done. It is remotely like all of your apps open, sucking the life out of your battery. But in this case, your mental to-do list is sucking the life out of effectiveness.

In order to be truly effective and efficient, having a daily schedule that systemizes what needs to be done is a game changer. It's worth repeating: *You don't have to be organized to have an organized system; you simply need to create the system and then follow through with it as it is written.*

As soon as this same client spent several weeks with me working on this system, he had a new perspective.

"Being able to see my work in one snapshot, as well as when I will do it, allows me to now create longer and more focused work periods. It matters greatly."

Organizing your daily schedule can have so many layers that I think we need to give each layer its own space. The endless options on ways to organize can be overwhelming as well, so it's critical to break this down into smaller parts.

Let's begin with those of you that know there must be a better way to schedule your life. Those that can see that not everyone is running around scratching their head every time an appointment is missed and that clearly, with the zillions of apps available, there must be a simpler method.

Let's begin with . . . you!

Creating an effective day
The key piece in being an organized thinker is to first create intention. We need a reason to think like an organized person. Just like any new commitment we are about to begin, the one reason we often try and fail over and over again is that we aren't clear about why we even want to do this. We may have a moment of— *I really need to lose weight so I can fit in these jeans*— but it isn't more than that. There isn't true intention around the decision to create the change, which is why the change doesn't occur.

What is your why?
1 – Grab a piece of paper or open your *Notes* app in your phone and make a list of at least ten instances of how being unorganized is keeping you from having what you want in your life.
2 – Now make a list of ten instances where being more organized could change your life. It doesn't matter how small or large the effects may be; jot them down. Truthfully, if this is something you have yet to master in your life, you may not even be able to comprehend the positive effects it will have on your life, but you have to be able to at least imagine them before you can begin.

Now, you know why you must be diligent about this simple act of having intention surrounding daily organization, every morning and every night.

For the beginners, (if you are not a beginner, but need a better way, skip down to *Fine-Tuning*) let's keep this simple. Very simple. Remember, our intention is to simply create a system that allows you to be more effective and productive during the day, so let's just do that!

If you are currently using your calendar app in your phone to organize your day, that is a great start! But as you can see, it is not enough. If it were, you would feel balanced, organized, and effective, yet here you are.

Remember when we used planners? Yes, PLANNERS! Depending on your age, you may have different points of reference for this. If you are a millennial, what you may recall is being given a planner or agenda book to keep track of your homework assignments and notes each day in school. If you have long passed this age in life, you may go back to what I remember as the best days of my life, when I was gifted a *Day-Timer*.

Do you remember it? Did you have one? Was your life as magical as mine was when you had it? It was impossible to forget a thing, because everything was in it! It was a small but thick book that had space each day (by the hour) of everything you had to do and every appointment you had to attend and you could see two days at a time, so you could always keep an eye on tomorrow as you dabbled through today.

In the beginning of each month, it also had a month at a glance so you could plan ahead. And in the back of the book, there were some pages for notes as well as pages for contacts, since that was back in the day when we didn't have cell phones.

Those days are gone, but the good old days don't have to be!

The truth is that part of our chaos and inefficiencies is in part due to our overload of technology, which in theory should be helping us to become more effective, yet when not used carefully can and will do the opposite. The truth is, that in order to think like an organized person, we must surrender to the belief that we actually cannot expect our memory to hold onto everything and expect success.

Remember when I asked you to write down your *why*. I didn't ask you to think about it and try to hold that memory, but, instead, to write it down. That is because once it is written, it becomes sealed in your mind, as well as on paper. It releases the thoughts you have about it so that you don't have to keep thinking about it. And even if it doesn't become sealed in your mind, your brain can stop worrying and thinking about it because it knows it is written and can safely be found again.

Hence where your planner comes in!

I am going to recommend my all-time favorite planner. Honestly, I have tried every planner there is under the sun, and this one seemed like an answer to my prayers. However, you need a planner that fits your needs and the way you think, minus the chaos and the familiarity. This will not feel familiar.

Familiar is picking up your phone, seeing the schedule for the day in small colored rectangles, opening up each one to see more details, and not having a clue about what your actual to-do list looks like.

Familiar is not always effective. It is just familiar.

Eventually we all have to throw away those old shoes, no matter how comfortable they are. Now seems like the perfect time.

The Passion Planner is literally one of my favorite work tools. I do not work for the company, though I probably should, given how much I love it, but I do recommend it to everyone I work with. It may seem extravagant and way too large for those that are used to keeping all of their details in their phone, but it will create meaningful change.

Here are some of its highlights:

- Two pages for each monthly calendar of events.
- A two-page spread of the week at a glance.
- Timelines for each day from morning until night.
- Space for personal tasks due each week.
- Space for professional tasks due each week.
- Weekly place of infinite possibility that can be used for brainstorming on upcoming/new projects.
- Monthly reflection pages to declare the things that are working, as well as the things that you need to do differently.
- Many blank pages in the back of the book to free write, design, draft or strategically plan out the event. (This is great if you are working on many projects at one time!)

And that is just one style of a planner. What I recommend before even buying a planner is to create a template in a spiral notebook. Take out a ruler if you have to, but create the five days of the work week with enough space to be detailed about what needs to be done, as well as some space for tasks that need to get done, even if you don't know when you will do them yet. The idea would be to try this for a week—just to see if it helps clear your mind in a way that leads to you feeling more focused while working.

Try it out! When you see that it works, because it will, then head to the store and find the perfect planner. You do not have to make a special trip to Staples; the food stores and even CVS have them as well. Of course they do! All the organized thinkers use them.

15

SO MANY SHOES

So many shoes, so little time. Are you with me on this one? I know it may seem ridiculous that there is a chapter about organizing your shoe collection, but keep remembering that the way we do one thing is the way we do everything. So if, in fact, that is true, then we should give our shoes the same time and space we do everything else.

Even if you live on your own and are not in fact a shoe hoarder (sometimes I wonder if I am getting close to that), you probably have more shoes than you are aware of. I mean, you have shoes for different seasons, right? Even my twenty-two-year-old son, who is not a collector of anything, has several pairs of shoes.

If you are an athlete or participate in any kind of exercise, you have different shoe wear for those activities. Maybe a pair of hiking boots for the trails, running sneakers, sneakers you can wear out to the movies, dress shoes, your *fancy* sneakers. You get the point. And then, if you honestly look deeper and consider indoor and outdoor shoes as well as seasonal, you may realize you have plenty to organize. Even with six pairs of shoes, you will see how having a system for them can create a mindful (and helpful) space in your brain and home that you didn't even know you needed.

How we do one thing is how we do everything
Why do we need a system for our shoes? Quite honestly, you don't *need* a system for anything. But the longer you deny that things in your life are not orderly and sometimes border on chaotic, the worse the problem will continue to be.

So let's take the small amount of time it will take to fix this seemingly unimportant task and get those feet in order.

Think about it. Your shoes should be treated with the utmost care. Your shoes. You place them on your feet every single day. They help you get from here to there and have been through the good days and the bad. They have helped your feet stay warm when all around you was cold and have consistently protected you (or at least your feet) from harm. I would go a bit farther and even say that they often can be a contribution to a good day or bad day.

Ever wear the *wrong* shoes all day long?

Remember, you do not have to be organized to keep track of your shoes. You just have to create a system for your shoes and then follow through with the system you have created.

There are some simple ways to get your shoes organized, and depending on how many pairs you have, it may not take long to do it. Yet no matter how many pairs you own, once this system is set in place, you will be gifted with time and space—knowing that you will no longer have to search for missing shoes or sanity.

First things first
Gather all of your shoes! I mean, ALL of them. Do you wear slippers in the house, slipper socks? Find them all. Grab your summer wear. Flip flops, sandals, spring shoes, etc. Don't forget the shoes you wear to work, athletic shoes, and all of your winter shoes and boots. Get them all out of the hidden spaces they are stashed away in.

Line them all up, then group by season
It makes sense to put them in groups according to which season they are worn. If you live in an area that has seasonal weather changes, no need

to have ALL of them accessible all year long. This just creates unnecessary clutter. We have enough clutter in our head, so let's not add to it with simple things like shoes we don't wear.

Let's pause before we get to the organizing part since we may be able to declutter a bit more. When you began to group your shoes by season, what did you find? Did you find a pair that you have loved since the beginning of time, but have noticed that the heel has worn badly on one side? Or maybe a once-favorite pair of workout shoes that you wore religiously, that may look fine, but no doubt have worn out on the inside in a way that are unsafe to work out in any longer?

If so, it is time to let go! If they are in really bad shape, go ahead, throw them out! But if it still looks decent and could serve someone else in need, go to your local donations box and toss them in. Someone would probably love to walk a mile in your shoes, so let's gift them that while gifting yourself a clear head space.

The organized thinker knows the importance of a box
If you are currently in the middle of winter, label the box: *Seasonal.*

Then fill it up with everything that you do not wear in the middle of winter. The reason we label it seasonal is so that you can use the same box over and over again as the seasons change. If you are tight on space, be creative. The garage (even if filled) is a great place to add a high shelf for things that you do not need to reach for more than once or twice a year.

If you don't have a garage, check all of your closets and see if there is one that might have a spot for a high shelf as well. If, even after deep digging, you can't find a space for a shelf, buy a large, rectangular, clear plastic box with a lid, which you can slide under a bed or couch once filled.

Remaining shoes
There are many simple and inexpensive ways to store your shoes, rather than just throwing them into the closet.

Shoe rack. They make simple shoe racks that are completely adjustable depending on the size of your closet, as well as the number of shoes you have.

Closet Maid. Closet Maid makes several different shoe solutions. There are shoe cubbies that can be hung in a closet if there is not enough floor space. Or shelving that can be continuously added to as more space is needed.

Over the door. There are many shoe holders that can hang on the inside of any closet, which is an easy, inexpensive, and space-saving solution.

Once you have found the best solution for your space, commit to keeping it organized. Promise yourself that every time you walk in the door, you will simply take that one pair of shoes and place it in the correct space. It will take an extra twenty seconds perhaps, even when exhausted, but will eliminate having to reorganize this space ever again. Until you need new shoes of course!

16

THE GARAGE

In my house, the garage is the one place that can turn into a complete mess in a matter of minutes. I am not sure if it is because, as a family, we are less concerned about its look or if, when we are searching for something, we are reckless in the search, but it happens often. And while even I am fine with a messy garage, it is the home for the important things we need at unusual times and it could not only cost time looking for the items, but also money. How many times have you given up on searching and then found it the second you come home with the new one?

It is no surprise that I am the finder in the house because, even in the garage, when I am done with a tool, back it goes to its previous spot. Unfortunately, not all of my tribe practices organized thinking. But they should!

Imagine how nice it would be if, on a whim, you decided you wanted to paint the bedroom, went to the garage, and was able to pull out all the tools needed to get started? Right away!

Or, maybe you don't know because that has never happened before?

When we have organized thoughts, we save time, money, and sanity so that we can live a more balanced and happy life. That is why you are reading this book right now.

So, let's go back to the garage.

It is pretty simple and also similar to the Memory Card Game. All you have to do is think of it in terms of what matches. In this case, though, you will need to think of things in terms of what, when, and where.

If the garage is the major part of your storage, you probably have random things in there that you do not even know you have. That is where we start.

Assess

Plan on spending an entire day pulling everything off the shelves. I know, this sounds like a nightmare, especially since you do not enjoy being organized, but think of it in terms of efficiency. If you take everything out and find that you don't need any of it, great! Call your favorite donation spot and have them pick it up.

Whallah! The garage will now be useful for your car or a great place to build your own workout room.

However, I am sure that isn't the case and, in fact, would beg to differ that you will be surprised by what you do have in there and how many you have of each item. If so, consider having a garage sale or setting a date for a donation pickup. Less is more.

Group: What, When, Where
What

As you go through everything in the garage, find your matches! What goes together? Are you a family of sports players or fans?

Great, put all the helmets, baseball gloves, bats, etc., in one group on the driveway.

Next, gather all the balls—footballs, tennis balls, lacrosse balls, etc.

Every time you find a match and group, make a mental note that you will never have to search for a tennis ball again!

When

Once you are done matching the obvious *what* items, move onto the *when* items. You may want to match all items that are related to a particular season. If you live in an area that has many seasons, group the winter, spring, summer, and fall items with the appropriate season.

Do you have fixer-up things? If you have paint, paint brushes, random knobs, pieces of wood scraps, etc., put them all together. Pay attention to what you have but keep in mind that since you are *matching*, you don't need to remember what you have, just which corner it is in.

Where

This one is a game-changer. As you now begin putting things back into the garage, consider when certain things are used. If the sporting gear is used all year long, for example, put them in a place that you and your family can access effortlessly.

If you rarely attempt fixer upper tasks, put those items away from the doors, and maybe even up on a shelf, so it doesn't take up space for the things you need to use daily. High shelves are a great use of space for things not needed often and help declutter the garage so you can find what you need more quickly.

I like to keep things like the tools and cleaning supplies close to the garage door since we use those items often. Since they can't all be right near the door and I don't want to put shoes on to grab a simple cleaning product, I have narrow throw rugs (yes, in the garage!) as a walking path to them. No shoes needed!

The organized thinker operates in a mindful way so that they can spend more time doing and less time thinking. And it has some obvious perks as you can now enjoy the downtime by pulling out the bat and glove when you son asks if you want to have a catch!

17

RETHINKING THE TO-DO LIST

The way we write lists, in a linear fashion, filling up an entire sheet of paper with all of the things we need to get done now, yesterday, soon, or today is so helpful! It is. However, the only thing that is helpful about it is that we have dumped our thoughts out onto paper so we can release our thoughts about. But, that is helpful because the thoughts surrounding what we need to do next is what often causes us anxiety and stress, making us less and less productive.

Having said that, while it is helpful to create the list and I highly recommend it, it also can be counterintuitive.

Think about that page you have just filled. If you counted all of the lines you have filled, how many tasks do you have to complete? Are there one hundred? Maybe there are more than you would like to count, so maybe you shouldn't. The important question is: *How does the list make you feel?*

Do you feel nervous, anxious, worried? Do you immediately jump into action, starting with numbers one to ten and begin checking them off? Or do you suddenly feel like you need to lie down?

If you are able to complete one to ten right away, then good for you! Because typically, the tasks that we list first, the ones that come rolling off the tips of our pens first, are the ones we keep putting off. As a matter of fact, my experience with clients is that most people continue to write the most important tasks down but continue stepping over them and excusing why they can't be done now.

They either stay on the list unchecked, or for those of you that are super organized, they chronically get moved to the next day. And then the next day. And then the next day.

When does it finally get done? Is it in the middle of the night, right before it is due? Or do you find yourself bargaining for more time on certain important tasks?

Either way you look at it, there are more productive ways to manage your to-do list and, surprise, surprise, they all involve organized thinking.

Let's start with the example of a large project due in a week. The reason you may continuously add this to tomorrow's to-do list is that simply seeing it feels too overwhelming to even begin. It is a very involved project that has layer after layer after layer.

That is why we avoid it. It's too much to even think about, especially the way it is written.

Our brain can think in a linear fashion when writing out tasks or trying to remember organized events, but when it comes to larger, more challenging tasks, there are so many pieces involved that a linear list just isn't that helpful.

Let's pick an event: Staff Holiday Party. If we begin a list, it could go on for several pages, because our thinking for this is all over the place. Each idea that comes up triggers another idea that may or may not actually go next.

Often, with larger projects I need to complete, like creating a workshop, for example, my brain tends to fire neurons (or tasks) faster than I can write. Every second that I think of one more thing that needs to be done, another one comes up, which creates another one and so on! Then, when I want to begin and go to look at this list, I don't even want to start.

Yet here is a simple way to create an overview of the tasks at hand. A bird's eye view of sorts so that you can see each task, as well as tasks that come off of those tasks.

Use each of these boxes as a different task. As you list one, think about what other thoughts pop up related to that one. Write that one near the other one. Keep doing that until all of your tasks are written.

As you fill in the boxes, connect them with an arrow. These connections will help you better organize time and space needed for all of these tasks.

Once that is complete, you will be able to look at the tasks at hand with more purpose. If there are several boxes that also have many details attached, create a new grid just for one of those larger projects. Then go through the same process in listing all the things that need to be done in each box and how they are connected.

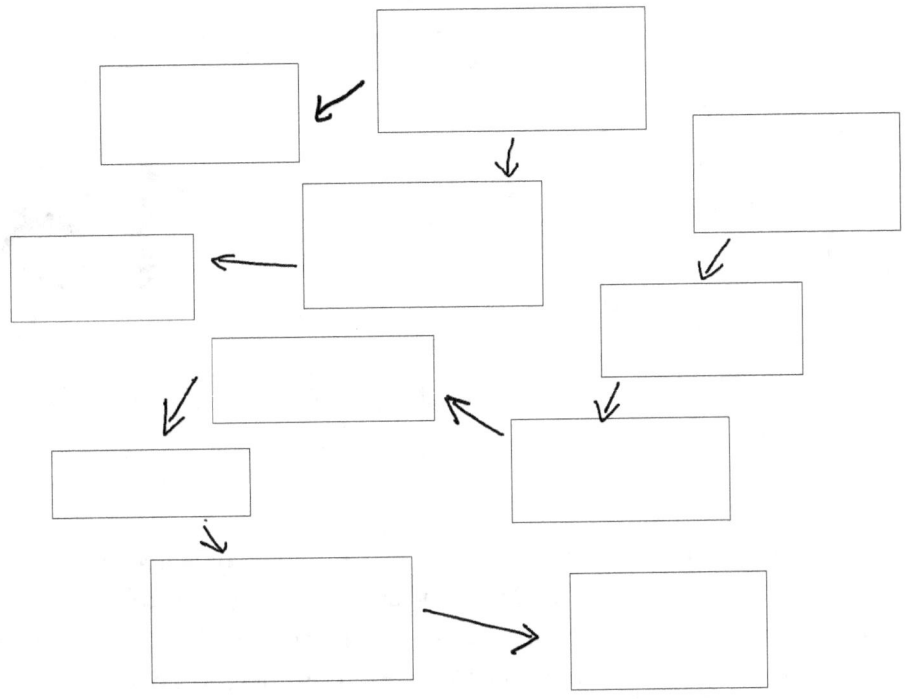

The point is to be able to look successfully at what needs to get done and be able to begin. Because, after all, in order to start anything, we simply need to begin!

18

FINE-TUNING THE DAILY LIST

There is nothing more frustrating than having a finely tuned list at the start of the day, only to realize that by the end of the day, half the list is still untouched. It is not that you are unorganized (maybe?). But some of you are! So why does this continue to happen even on the good days?

The most common answer people give is that unexpected things in their life are constant distractions. *You have no idea how my life is!*

I probably do. With four children now aged between fifteen and twenty-six, periods of life as a single parent, many years of working three jobs at a time, with my head constantly on a swivel . . . I probably do. What I know is that it is not so much about what comes at us, but how we think and respond to what comes at us.

We actually have more control of our day than we want to believe. I mean, let's face it, if we believed it was mostly in our control, wouldn't that then mean that we were the ones to blame for not getting things done? However, the fact that you have started a day thinking you were off to a solid start with a great list is a very good beginning! We certainly can't accomplish anything until we have an understanding of what needs to be done. So all we need to do now is finely tune how the list is made and the action steps to follow.

The organized thinker knows what to do, knows where and how to write a complete task list, and follows the same protocol for following through with success.

Compartmentalizing the list

1. List everything that needs to get done this week. You can also look at the grid you made from the previous chapter that shows all of the tasks.
2. Organize the tasks by day. Keep it simple by writing an 'M' next to anything that you want to complete on Monday, a 'T' next to the tasks for Tuesday, etc.

    The next step is to figure out when and how they will get done. It is not enough to say, *I will finish that on Monday*. While it may sound helpful, there is a reason for daily lists that do not get completed. So, let's take it a step further.
3. Starting at the top of the list, assess all the tasks you want completed on Monday.
4. Next to each task, write the approximate amount of time it will take to complete. Round up! If you think you can complete it in ninety minutes, write two hours. The goal is to design a schedule that fosters success. Period. The wiggle room of extra time will be a game changer.
5. Next, put a star next to any one task that is either very challenging, constantly avoided, or needs a great deal of attention.

    Now you are ready to fill in your planner. You do have a planner, right? If not, get one or make one. If you can't do either of those right now, start working with your Google calendar.
6. As you begin to place these tasks into your planner or calendar, fill in the ones you have marked with a star first and add them to a time during the day that you consider your most focused time of day.
7. Account for the time you think you will actually need, with the cushion, and add it to your planner. If you have a task that could

take ninety minutes and you decide you are most focused at 9 a.m., then block out the calendar from 9-11 a.m. and write in that task.

8. If there are tasks that could take four hours, and you know you can only sit for two hours at a time, then look at the whole day and whole week. Can you schedule it for two-hour sittings in one day? Or are you able to separate it into two different days?

   Be specific as well as mindful of what works for you. Account for your family life, work like, and how your brain works best. Do not schedule based on the way you wish you could work. Base it on how you currently work.

9. Lastly, if an emergency comes up and something has to go by the wayside, don't assume you will do it later. Get your pen, look at the calendar, and write it in for the next best time. Don't skip this part.

10. Lastly, have fun with it! It's detailed and may feel overwhelming at first, but the planning is the most challenging part (because it is unfamiliar). However, it will make the *doing* part feel easy because you will spend less time thinking and more time doing.

19

INCREASE YOUR BOTTOM LINE

Evolving into an organized thinker involves more than simply neatening stacks of papers and sliding it all into your desk drawer at the end of each day. The organized thinker creates systems and procedures for each part of the business, intuitively fostering productivity and financial growth.

Start small, with one tip at a time, until you feel you can comfortably incorporate it into a new, sustainable, organizational process. Once it becomes automatic, move onto the next tip!

Remember that it is our *thinking* that makes our doing easier.

1 – *Organization of papers*
Paper is the biggest disorganization culprit for most of us, so let's start there. If you don't have a filing system and/or a digital archiving system in place, now is the time to build one. Start by taking a look at the papers you have laying around. Make a *keep* pile and a *discard* pile, then shred or recycle all of the papers, magazines, newsletters, cards, notes, etc., that made it to the second pile. Before being able to go through the *keep* pile, you will need a place for them. Three-tiered, stackable trays are a simple way to create a sustainable system, as well as standing or hanging files.

Once you have a place for these, go back to the *keep* pile and put that into three small piles, labeling them: Now, Tomorrow, File, which should correlate to the trays or folders you just created. By starting and ending each day with this simple, organized thinking trick, not only will your desk be organized, but your mind will be less cluttered as well.

If you decide it's time to start moving toward a paperless office, then you can start by scanning in and digitizing your receipts, using online invoicing and payment services, and moving to a digital signature.

If you collect business cards at events during the year, it may also be a good idea to invest in a business card scanner so you can digitize contact info immediately and ditch the paper cards.

2 – Productivity tools
While we have favorite apps and tools we use every day, we should take stock of the apps we use every few months, and decide if they are still useful. This is also a great time to consider if you have some gaps and may need to invest in new productivity apps.

These business topics can easily be managed with apps:

Contact management
Meetings and communication
Accounting and bookkeeping
Travel and expense tracking
Social media management
E-mail management
Project management.

Productivity is a very personal process, and the apps you need will be specific to you the work you do and the way you tend to work. Take time to explore what your needs are before incorporating a new tool in your process. You may not need as many as you think, and too many tools can create overload as well.

3 – Get your computer organized
As a small business owner who does most of his/her work on the computer, this one is very important. It doesn't take long for your desktop to become cluttered with icons and your downloads folder to get filled with strangely-named documents. It can quickly become impossible to find anything. If you combine that to an overloaded inbox, your computer can actually become a source of contention each morning. This will hinder your productivity.

Here are some simple tasks to clean up your computer so it fosters, rather than hinders, productivity:

Clean up your desktop
It may take some time to do, but it will it will save you hours of time throughout each week, so it will be well worth that time.

Update software
If your computer is set to automatically install the application and operating system updates, great. If it's a manual process for you, you should check for updates at least bi-monthly. Then, once a year, review the current versions of software you are using and decide if it's time to upgrade.

Verify the integrity of your data backup
You are backing up your data, right? If not, skip everything else for the time being and do this one first. You can either use a cloud-based data backup service or you can use an external hard drive that you plug into your computer.

Create an inbox system
As small business owners, we love our inbox because it's a highly productive and efficient communication tool, yet hate it because it quickly gets out of control, causing unnecessary stress. However, with some simple systems, stress can be removed and efficiency can be increased. Try limiting how often you check e-mail during the day, designate times of day to

respond to e-mails needing attention, and create folders to keep organized those files that need attention in the future.

The above tips will help you become more efficient, effective, and productive immediately, but in order for it to be sustainable, you will need to attend to each of these as part of your daily system. Take it slow. Try them one at a time. Remember that everything is a simple mindset shift. Once you begin to feel the results, you will wonder how you survived before doing these simple tasks.

20

YOUR HEALTH AND NEGATIVE THINKING

We have to plant our feet and get a grip here. Yes, the Coronavirus has not only gripped our lives, but it seems to be changing the trajectory of where each of us will go next. Not being able to fly home, sports seasons ending before scouts have been able to see a game, offices being closed, schools . . . the list goes on and on. And people are surely in a panic. Not only are people panicked but many are consumed with so much negative thinking that they can barely see straight.

Panic, while reasonable in times like these, is not helpful
This is not our first rodeo with outrageous, disturbing, or life-threatening events that leave us feeling powerless, and no doubt will not be our last, but we still need a place to feel grounded.

What we really need during a crisis of this sort is a place to stand that can keep us healthy in mind, body, and spirit. While knowledge is power and easy to get every time you turn on the TV, some things are not as easy to access but even more important. The most powerful thing to access right now is a way to overcome these negative thought patterns.

"This is going to be so so bad. This is getting worse by the minute. We are all going to be quarantined. How will the kids get to graduate? So many of us are going to die! There won't be enough room in the hospitals for all the people that are going to get sick!"

While these feelings may very well become truths, there are some things to note. Not everyone ran to the store to buy as much toilet paper as possible, yet many did. Don't get me wrong; I prefer an overload of toilet paper in the house on a good day, so that is why I didn't run to the store, but there's more to it than that. While everyone is experiencing this crisis, not everyone is experiencing the same feeling surrounding it.

We don't see things as they are. We see things as WE are

We view the world through our mental attitude. And while in most cases it is fine that we all see things differently, being consumed with negative thoughts can actually impact everything, including your health, career, family, and more! Not only that, but it can have a spiraling effect that attracts more negative thinking.

During this crisis of the Coronavirus, or any crisis, we need to pause, take a breath, and maybe even turn off the news for just a few minutes. These constant negative external and internal cues are making the panic even worse.

The only thing worse than a pandemic, is panic
Transform negative thinking before it begins to make you sick by training yourself to think differently with some simple tips.

1. **Have daily negative thought time**
   Yes, you heard right! You are going to allow yourself the time to vent by committing ten minutes a day to ruminate about whatever negativity is on your mind. It must be ten minutes. And it must be every day. If you have a negative thought later in the day, have a journal handy and jot it down. After a few days of this activity, your brain will begin to understand that anything on this list will be given its time during the next negative thought time.
2. **Reframe the negative thoughts**

We will never eliminate negative thinking because it is a normal thought process. Yet what we can do is simply replace it with more mindful and productive thoughts. When it begins to occur, pause.
- a. Notice what triggered this pattern of thinking.
- b. Acknowledge that this is exactly what you want to change.
- c. Say aloud what you want to be thinking about instead.
- d. Flip the commentary and find a positive focus.

3. **Be good to yourself**
Nearly 90 percent of self-talk is negative and is the opposite of being kind.
- a. *Let it out*. Yep, out! *Give yourself three minutes and then end the pity party.*
- b. *Jot it down*. *Notice what triggers you into this negative thinking and jot it down in a journal or notebook. Awareness will become your new trigger into positive thoughts.*
- c. *Reframe it*. *Once you hear it, shift your head to the side and put your thoughts into a new frame. What would you say to your best friend?*

4. **More doing, less thinking**
Research shows that when we can write out our thoughts, we are more inclined to let them go. In addition, just seeing the words on a page makes it easier to digest and move forward.

5. **Make a gratitude list**
Every morning, while you are sipping on your morning coffee or tea, find the things you are grateful for. It's a game changer. Remember that your mind is in charge. So give it some direction!

6. **Create a few reflective questions**
- a. How do I feel with this negative commentary?
- b. What do I lose by being consumed with these thoughts?
- c. How could I benefit from changing this commentary?

7. **Eliminate negative influences**
Stop watching the morning news. Research has shown that just three minutes of negative news in the morning will significantly increase your chances of negative feelings all day long.

8. **Develop a morning ritual**

    One of the easiest and most effective ways to stop the noise is to create a ritual that you can stick to every morning when you first open your eyes. I recommend starting with something simple like changing the alarm sound on your phone. Instead of the standard beeping sound, set it to play a song that you love, one that sends a positive message, offers hope, makes you smile. Then commit to listening to the whole song before even getting up, thereby filling your head with positive thoughts.

9. **Turn negative thinking into constructive thoughts**

    Have a prepared positive thought process ready to go when the negative thinking takes over. Maybe there is an event coming up that you are excited about. Maybe just the simple thought of your dog giving you unconditional love. Or maybe the thought of your beautiful children. Then, any time something negative comes up, notice it and commit to switching your thoughts to something that makes you smile.

10. **Commit to exercise and meditation**

    If you already have both of these in your life, perfect. If you don't, let's design that starting today. Perhaps you can't be in the gym every time your brain switches to negative thinking, but taking a mindful minute can be done anywhere and a quick walk around the block can change everything.

We can't escape negative thoughts completely, but if we are able to disrupt the thought process, they will be less likely to take over your day and your life. The organized thinker knows that people with positive dispositions get sick less and live longer. So why not try this on? It may feel difficult at first, but if you do it consistently, your brain will begin to talk itself out of this thinking without much effort at all.

Mindset is a choice, so let's start choosing something that we can happily spread around, especially when times get tough.

21

ACCOUNTABILITY

There are three important stages of accountability—establishing strengths; designing daily, monthly, and weekly timelines; and creating a support system.

Definition:
The obligation of an individual or organization to account for its activities, accept responsibility for them, and to disclose the results in a transparent manner.

Accountability is by far the biggest challenge busy professionals face when pursuing their goals. With a lack of structure and clear path to achieving goals, almost everything can stand in the way of success.

When taking a closer look at your own accountability, it's important to take the time needed to figure out what works and what doesn't. It's important to be brutally honest as well. Take the time now to grab a pen and answer these questions.

Establishing personal accountability strengths and weaknesses

1. What are your strengths in the area of accountability (areas at home or work when you are able to hold yourself accountable)?

1. When do you find it most difficult to hold yourself accountable?
2. What strategies do you currently use to hold yourself accountable?
3. Who do you turn to for support? What works about the relationship? What does not work about the relationship?

Now that you have assessed your weaknesses and strengths in this area, you are ready to design some accountability goals.

Creating accountability goals with a purpose

In order to be truly accountable, we need a purpose as well as detailed and reasonable plans on how to complete our goals. Without these, our goals become just thoughts distracting us from productivity.

1 – Name one long-range goal that is important to you or your business.
2 – Name three to five goals that need to be accomplished in order for the long-range goal to be completed. (#1, 2, 3, 4, 5)
3 – Name one goal for each of the three to five goals listed in the above question. (#1a, 2a, 3a, etc.)
4 – Now go back to each goal and add a 'frequency' of task, and/or due date.
5 – Next to each goal, add the initials of a person who can help support you in this area.

Long Range Goals:

Related Goals (3-5)	Frequency of task	By when
1.		
1a		

Related Goals (3-5)	Frequency of task	By when
2.		
2a		
3.		
3a		
4.		
4a		
5.		
5a		

Examples:

Related Goals (3-5)	Frequency of task	By when
1. Lucrative monthly sales		Month/date/year
1a. cold calls, set appts 1b. follow up on leads 1c. close the sale	Daily/Weekly Daily/weekly Weekly/Monthly	

Related Goals (3-5)	Frequency of task	By when
2. Successful branding		Month/date/year
2a. update website 2b. strategize marketing plan	Monthly	Month/date/year
3. Established positive relationships with clients		Month/date/year
3a. communication with clients (e-mail, calls)	weekly	
4. Efficient and prompt organizational system		Month/date/year
4a. prompt filing, organizing and updating client data	Daily, Weekly	
5.		
5a		

22

BUSINESS SYSTEMS

As busy professionals we face a common problem—too much to do and too little time.

As a business owner or entrepreneur, this problem prevents business growth as time is spent working on (not in) the business, and eventually leads to burnout.

The answer to this problem lies in systems. Are you beginning to see a pattern here? The organized thinker understands that having a system in place creates balance everywhere.

The way we do one thing is the way we do everything (or at least most things).

In this scenario, a system is a method of solving a repeated business issue in a strategic and effortless way, helping you to work smarter, not harder.

Although we may always feel the pinch of time and the stress of our job, we don't have to suffer needlessly with tasks that can be systematized.

If we can do it in the overwhelming and unorganized garage, we can definitely do it here.

While you may have created some systems without realizing it, the best systems are designed intentionally, so you're able to replicate it in other areas as well.

Here are some qualities of a system:

- A system addresses a specific problem or business issue.
- A system is automatic.
- Once created, a system does not require intensive thought or effort.
- A system is a process or routine.

The benefits of systems
Business growth. The overriding impact of a system is that it can cause a business to grow. Instead of reacting to a crisis, you can proactively address growth hurdles. When you implement the right systems, you create for yourself both more time and mental freedom. With this time and mental energy, you can work to grow your business instead of burying yourself in busy work.

Systems save time. A simple system, once created and acted upon, can save hundreds of hours each year.

Systems dodge problems. In business, small problems can eventually lead to massive ones. Putting systems in place can successfully deal with small-scale problems, helping to avoid looming future problems.

Systems improve productivity. Improving your business isn't just about saving time. It's about using the time you have to the greatest possible advantage. That's the power of productivity.

What can you systematize?
You can systematize major business issues such as bookkeeping, and you can systematize smaller issues such as stocking your snack room. Here is how to find issues that need systems:

- Identify issues that happen regularly. Example: Invoicing
- Identify issues that take a lot of time. Example: Tax preparation
- Identify issues that frustrate you. Example: Daily commute

- Identify issues that are outside of your core competency. Example: Cleaning

The organized thinker will even systematize meal preparation to help effortlessly enjoy healthy meals every day. It requires more thought at first, but once it becomes habit, planning out a menu for the week and having foods readily available just begins to make sense.

Once the system is in place, the stress is gone, the hurdle is obliterated, and the distraction dissolves.

A simple process to create a business system:

Identify your issue. Pick something to systematize. Does it happen regularly, require a lot of time, or frustrate you? If so, then start to systematize it.

Plan your process. A system is basically a sophisticated process. You must plan exactly what this process is going to look like. A well-defined process solves your issue in a sequential way. I recommend that you write down the process by enumerating each of the steps. In some cases, you will want to outsource some or all of the process.

Execute your plan. Having a plan isn't the same as acting on your plan. Now it's time to execute. You may need to hire help. If you are systematizing housecleaning, you may need to hire a maid service. If you are systematizing workplace safety, you may need to hire an occupational health and safety consultant. With other systems, you might need to simply follow your plan. The first few times you may have to read from your numbered list as you follow the plan. Eventually, the system becomes a routine, allowing you to effortlessly overcome what used to be time-consuming problems.

Setting up a system on the front end takes quite a bit of time. In the long run, however, you're saving yourself hundreds of hours of frustration and stress and will feel balanced and organized, even if the desk is still somewhat messy.

Sample systems:

- **E-mail systems.** Use a schedule to check e-mails, write e-mails, and file e-mails.
- **Hiring systems.** Follow a consistent process for finding, screening, hiring, and onboarding new hires.
- **Cleaning systems.** Develop a routine that allows you or a third-party service to clean your office space.
- **Scheduling systems.** Create a system by which people can find available times on your calendar and schedule a meeting with you.
- **Meeting systems.** Come up with a plan for taking notes during meetings, creating actionable steps in that meeting, and following up on the execution of those steps.
- **Accounting systems.** Work with a bookkeeper or accountant to efficiently process receivables and payables.
- **Travel systems.** Streamline the process of scheduling, finding airline tickets, arranging airport pickup, and reserving accommodations.
- **Wardrobe systems.** Eliminate the need for time-consuming shopping or the mentally demanding task of choosing what clothes to wear each day.

Systems are the ultimate method of turning a struggling business into a well-oiled machine. You can systematize virtually anything in your business. Every single system has the potential to reduce your mental load, free up time, overcome hurdles, enhance your progress, and create success in a sustainable way.

23

PROCRASTINATION

What is all of this procrastinating actually about? Why am I so unmotivated at times, putting things off for as long as possible, and then jumping into action at other times with no real thought at all?

The answer may be more obvious than you really want to hear.

In general, we tend to procrastinate on things, well, that we just don't feel like doing. Ugh. That may not be the answer you were hoping for. That's pretty obvious!

But the larger question at hand: How do we change that or how do we have more control on it that so we can be more efficient in getting stuff done? Especially the things we keep putting off!

First, what we need to do is to find a starting point. You need to look at when you procrastinate most often.

- Is there a certain time of day?
- Is it a particular project that always gets put on the backburner?
- Is there a day of the week when you feel the least motivated?
- Are there any triggers that are associated with this feeling?

It is important to pinpoint one area at a time, since procrastination is not generally an arch covering all the parts of your life, every day.

I will give two examples of procrastination pain points that I have walked through with many of my clients, and then help peel off the layers, so you can actually get into action.

Procrastination 1: Waking up

Do you find that, on most mornings, the alarm sounds and you hit the snooze button once, twice, maybe even three or four times?

If so, it is time to lose the snooze! That button should not have been created. Let's think about it. The alarm goes off, your brains says, *I'm exhausted,* you then hit the snooze. Makes sense, right? I mean, if you are tired, a little more sleep is just what you need.

However, if you think about it, this concept does not make sense at all.

Let's say you have just slept eight hours. The alarm wakes you from a deep sleep, the brain says *no*, and you are certain that another seven minutes will do the trick. Or, for some of you, twenty-one more minutes will do the trick, even with being woken up twice more in between.

What happens the last time the alarm goes off? Do you feel energized? Ready to start the day? Do you feel finally rested that very last time? Doubtful. So tomorrow, when the alarm goes off, before you touch the snooze, ask yourself these questions:

- Did I have enough sleep last night?
- Could I be fighting a cold, cough, etc., and need more sleep?
- Have I been working out harder than normal?
- Am I feeling anxious or stressed by something in particular?

If you haven't slept well, are not feeling well, or have exhausted your body more than usual, I recommend not hitting the snooze, but instead, resetting the alarm for another thirty minutes of sleep. Then at least, you will get some extra rest.

If you had plenty of sleep, are feeling well, and should be able to get up, then try to figure out what you are avoiding and fix that, instead of hitting the snooze.

Maybe you need to create a different morning ritual

- If you normally wake up to young children who are hungry and needy, consider setting the alarm for a time that is at least fifteen minutes before they get up. I know it is hard, since you are tired, but waking up to *your* time line, rather than someone else's needs, is much more motivating.
- When the alarm sounds, grab a quick shower to help get the body going.
- Find a quiet spot to sit and sip a cup of tea or coffee.
- Like to read? Have your book right beside your bed and stay cozy under the covers for a few more minutes while reading.

The idea is to give yourself a reason to wake up! Truthfully, your body will always feel tired for at least a few minutes when being asked to transition between sleep and wake mode, so let's try easing into it.

Procrastination #2: Tasks/work projects
What is it about specific projects that make us delay over and over again?

To answer that question, we need to first acknowledge that you are not just simply lazy. I mean, there are plenty of things you do efficiently and effectively all day long, so how could that possibly be true? Once you settle into that truth, you can lower your shoulders and begin to uncover what is beneath this avoidance.

Each thing we are avoiding seems to have its own layer, so it is important to keep doing this activity any time avoidance comes up. It's important because when you are working to solve a problem, your brain can stay in action and create forward movement. For instance, like choosing to read this book, even though this lack of organization has almost become your way of life. You decided (for whatever reason) that you are tired of your current method of doing things and then made a decision to do something to change. A solution.

It's also important to keep peeling away the layers of why this project is being avoided, because the more you resist it, the more it slows you down. You know that every time you secretly put *that* project in that invisible box called *later*, your brain is silently fixated on what you are not doing. And any negative self-talk at all interferes with productivity. It's that simple.

The organized thinker does not participate in self-sabotage.

How well do you know yourself?

Think about a particular project you are currently (or already have been) avoiding.

- List why you don't want to do this project.
- It is too large a project?
- Is it something that does not interest you?
- Are you unclear where to start?

Let's assume it is all of them combined—too large, not that interesting, has many layers in it, and you don't know where to start. That feels like the perfect storm for avoidance! So just a few more questions and we can get started on moving this boulder out of your way.

- Is there anyone else that you can delegate it to or recruit to help?
- Do you *have* to do it?
- Why was this task given to *you*?

I don't like to make assumptions, but most of my clients that have projects they are avoiding also report that the due date on completing them has already passed. Add that to the list of why we continue putting them in the *later* pile. I mean, it's already late. So what's the difference?

Actually, it matters greatly! The later it gets, the more disruptive it is, even when you think you don't care about it at all. It is and will continue to affect more and more tasks.

Let's break it down and look closely at this project. Yes, let's pull it out and actually look at it. Clear your desk and lay the project out. Move everything else onto the floor if need be. Don't worry, you don't have to complete it right now, but the goal is to look carefully at it to eliminate the fear surrounding it and create a brief action plan.

- Create a deadline for completion.
- Declare how many hours in total it will take to complete.
- Declare how long you can work in one sitting (be honest with yourself).

Make sure you answer the above questions honestly. If normally you can sit focused for ninety minutes on one task, account for two hours on this one, keeping in mind that it is not something you are motivated to do.

Now all you need to do is take the amount of time it will take to get it done and how long you can work in one sitting and then schedule it in your calendar. With reminders and alarms. Do not skip this part. Do not fool yourself into thinking that this time it will be different. It won't. Until you are able to actually put this into practice, your brain will continue to avoid it at all costs. Only the actual action of doing the work will change the way your brain responds and motivate you to complete it.

When scheduling it in your calendar, note what time of day you are most focused and be sure to schedule the work time for that time. If you know that right after your morning check in with coffee in hand is when you are most focused, schedule it then. It not only will help you complete the task at hand, but the rest of the day may even feel easy knowing you have begun to tackle this project.

The best to way start anything is to simply begin.

24

SCHEDULE SCRUPULOUSLY

Your future depends on your state of consciousness now.

—*Eckert Tolle*

What is your current state of consciousness? I mean, truly, what is going on for you right now, in this minute? Are you bargaining for time as you declare you are going to read this chapter? Or will you just skim it? Or are you in a relaxed state, aware of your commitments this minute and those ones out in front of you?

Your future depends on your state of consciousness now.

For some of you, as the words settle into your bones, you may be worried, since your *now* is not that good or at least not nearly what you would like it to be. You may be concerned because you have been counting on the future like some magical moment when all of your stars finally come into alignment and never realized that it was attached to *now*. But it is. Greatly attached, in fact.

The good news is that your future depends on your state of consciousness *now*, not simply on what is going on in your life right now. As human beings, we think those two things go together. We believe that what is going on in our life right now is actually causing our state of consciousness in this minute. We believe that what we are consciously thinking about is almost unconscious, in a way, because we believe we can't control it. We believe it is a result of things occurring in our life.

The reason I say that is good news is because those two things are not actually tied together at all. They are separate. There is what is occurring. And then there is how you perceive it. We like to wrap them up together and then strap it on our backs, giving us plenty to complain about as we walk around feeling rightfully upset and overwhelmed. But what if you could separate them?

Simple.

Let's look at the feeling of being overwhelmed. It is not just a feeling. Right? You are overloaded at work with deadlines, impatient co-workers, inefficient administrators, laundry, food shopping, and a family filled with needs. How could you possibly be anything but stressed out and overwhelmed? No one could manage all of that on their plate and actually feel calm and in control.

Actually, the overload of tasks has nothing to do with how you are feeling. You have consciously taken on *overload* as a feeling because you have not figured out a way to manage the list at hand. In continuing to allow that, you are also becoming inefficient in each and everything that you are attempting to complete right now. Even if you say you are an expert at multi-tasking, I would then ask: *Why do you feel so overwhelmed?*

So, let's take a closer look, because if in fact your future depends on your state of consciousness now, it will be important to alter that state. Now.

What can you do?
1 – Declare that you are in control of this thing you call life. Period.
2 – Get a notebook or planner that can always be with you.
3 – Write one complete list (with short descriptions) of all that needs to be done today.
4 – Write a separate list for things that need to be done on different days.
5 – For each task, write an estimated time of day that it can be completed.

6 – Look at the list as a whole and make sure it is reasonable to complete all the things listed.
7 – If the list is not reasonable, can you recruit someone to help you? Or is there a way to alter your schedule for the day or the week to accommodate this?
8 – Be creative! Be unreasonable!

That's the easy part! The more challenging part is to now begin to separate yourself from this list. This list is merely a reminder of things that need to be done. It is not a way of being. It is not what will predict your future. Whether you finish all of them, or some of them, will not affect your future success. What will affect it is the way you think about it in this present moment.

Our life is not about the stuff to do; it is about our stream of consciousness about it. It is why some people with no money are happy and why some with an abundance of money are not.

You have to choose.

Choose your state of consciousness—what you think about, how you think about it. Choose a way of being and feeling that makes you happy, that impacts you and those around you, regardless of what is actually *happening*. To-do lists are temporary, just as is your state of consciousness. So, choose it now. Then be prepared to choose it again in a few minutes. This simple process will have the largest impact on your future . . . the one where all the stars are aligned. The one that is actually available to you right now.

25

OFFICE ORGANIZATION

You may think that you don't have time to organize your office, but if you really knew how much time that disorganization was costing you, you would reconsider. Rearranging and moving piles occasionally doesn't count. Neither does clearing off your desk, if you swipe the mess into a bin or a desk drawer. A relatively neat and orderly office space clears the way for higher productivity and less wasted time.

Do not feel overwhelmed by this topic. The mere reason we need to have an office that is organized is because it fosters organized thinking. That is the only reason. Once we can put things where they belong, we can think clearly and that is the end game.

Organizing your office doesn't have to take days; it can be done a little at a time. In fact, maintaining an organized office is much more effective if you treat it like an ongoing project, instead of a massive assault. So, if you're ready to get started, the following tips will help you transform your office into an efficient workspace.

Tips to organize your office space

Purge your office
De-clutter, empty, shred, get rid of everything that you don't need or want. Look around. What haven't you used in a while? Take one area at a time.

If it doesn't work, send it out for repair or toss it. If you haven't used it in months and can't think of when you'll actually need it, out it goes. This goes for furniture, equipment, supplies, etc. Don't forget about knick-knacks, plants (real or artificial), and decorations—if they're covered with dust and make your office look shabby, they're fair game.

Gather and redistribute
Gather up every item that isn't where it belongs and put it where it does.

Establish work zones
Decide what type of activity happens in each area of your office. You'll probably have a main workspace (most likely your desk), a reference area (filing cabinet, shelves, binders), and a supply area (closet, shelves, or drawers). Place the appropriate equipment and supplies in the proper area as much as possible.

Close proximity
Position the equipment and supplies that you use most within reach. Things that you rarely use can be stored or put away.

Get a good labeler
Choose a label maker that's simple to use. Take the time to label shelves, bins, baskets drawers. Not only will it remind you where things go, but it will also help others who may have a need to find, use, or put away anything in your workspace.

Revise your filing system
Thanks to technology, the need to store paper files has decreased. Have you decreased your paper files? What can you store digitally? Are you duplicating files? You may be able to eliminate some of the files and folders you've used in the past. If you're storing files on your computer, make sure you are doing regular backups.

Here are some quick tips for creating a smooth filing system:

Create a meeting folder
Put all *items to be discussed* in there along with items that need to be handed off, reports that need to be given, etc. It will help you prepare for meetings and save you from feeling anxious in the event that a meeting is moved up.

Create a 'Waiting on Response' (WOR) folder
So much of our messy papers are things that are on hold until someone else responds or acts. Put them in a WOR (Waiting on Response) folder. Check it every few days for outstanding actions you may need to follow up on.

Clear off your desk
Remove everything, clean it thoroughly, and put back only those items that are essential for daily use.

Organize your desktop
Now that you've streamlined your desktop, it's a good idea to organize it. Use desktop organizers or containers to organize the items on your desk. Use trays for papers, containers for smaller items.

Organize your drawers
Put items used together in the same drawer space, stamps with envelopes, sticky pads with notepads, etc. Use drawer organizers for little items—paper clips, tacks, etc. Use a separate drawer for personal items.

Separate inboxes
If you work regularly with other people, create a folder, tray, or inbox for each.

Clear your piles
Hopefully with your new organized office, you won't create piles of paper anymore, but you still have to sort through the old ones. Go through the pile (a little at a time if necessary) and put it in the appropriate place or dump it.

Sort mail
Don't just stick mail in a pile to be sorted. Sort it as soon as you get it and organize it—to act, to read, to file, to delegate, or hand off.

Assign discard dates
You don't need to keep every piece of paper indefinitely. Mark on files or documents when they can be tossed or shredded. Some legal or financial documents must be kept for a specified length of time. Make sure you know what those requirements are.

Storage boxes
Use inexpensive storage boxes to keep archived files and get them out of your current file space.

Magazine boxes
Use magazine boxes or binders to store magazines and catalogs you really want to store. Please make sure you really need them for reference or research, otherwise recycle them or give them away.

Reading folder
Designate a file for print articles and documents you want to read that aren't urgent.

Archive files
When a project is complete, put all of the materials together and file them away. Keep your 'working folders' for projects in progress.

Straighten your desk
At the end of the day, do a quick straighten, so you have a clean start the next day.

File weekly
Don't let your filing pile up. Put your papers in a *To File* folder and file everything once a week.

Use one tip or try them all. The amount of effort you put into creating and maintaining an efficient work area will pay off in a big way. Instead of spending time looking for things and shuffling piles, you'll be able to spend your time *working*.

26

ELIMINATE E-MAIL OVERLOAD

E-mail was intended to save time, money, and energy. Unfortunately, for many, it causes undeniable stress and overload and, rather than helping professionals become more efficient in completing tasks, it often does the opposite.

Too many emails lead to feelings of overload and resistance.

An engineer client stated simply, "I have 29,000 unread e-mails. I get so many every day that I literally have stopped checking them."

"Are any of them important?" I asked. "Do you get e-mails that lay out tasks that administrators need you to complete?"

"Yes, but I also have dozens of half-written e-mail responses. Basically, by the time I am halfway through one, another ten come in, and I get side tracked. So, I stop writing and move onto something else."

An organized thinker knows that this solution will not lead to success. It is similar to the mess on your desk that you keep suggesting does not bother you. While that may or may not be true, the resistance to create an organized space continues to distract from all other tasks. Whether you admit it or not, your brain is on overdrive, hoping that you aren't missing something important.

Not only are you putting up with this mess of e-mail overload, but little by little, details will begin (if they haven't already) slipping through the cracks. When that happens, your accountability will come into question, as deadlines are missed.

There are many ways to create an e-mail system, but an important first step is in realizing that the system you have now is making you less efficient. You may fall into two categories:

- Do you answer as many e-mails as you can as often as possible?
- Do you check the inbox infrequently and scan for what might be important, doing little with all else?

If you fall into either of the above categories, making some slight changes will have a high payoff. Remember, you don't have to be organized to think like an organized person. You just need a simple system so that you can open your e-mail with intention.

The first way to do that is by treating *checking e-mail* like a task for the day. No more browsing in search of something interesting. Instead, each time you check the inbox with intention, you will be looking for three things:

- Which ones can you respond to in two minutes or less?
- Which ones can you delete?
- Which ones can be stored in folders for later?

When to check e-mail:
Clients often report that they have to check e-mail all day long, as quickly as it comes in, because clients want instant responses. Now, that may be true, depending on the business you are in, but typically, when we took the time to look at those specific e-mails, none were urgent at all. So, the first solution was to turn off the e-mail alerts.

Instead of incoming e-mail dictating your entire day, you regain the controls and declare when and how you will check the mail.

If you normally check e-mail every few minutes, try setting an alarm for every hour. Even that is most likely too often, but we want to begin with a process that you can begin with success. The timeliness of checking e-mail can be altered as needed, as long as you are the one declaring when. It should not be a distraction from other work, nor in the middle of a focus period you have chosen. It is so easy to turn to e-mail when we need a break from something, or as an excuse to not begin working on your least favorite (or most challenging) project. Resist the urge.

Intention:

Plan for about twenty-thirty minutes each time you check e-mail.

Look at each e-mail from the top down, in search of answering, deleting, or putting into a folder.

- Answering: During opening and closing times of business, answer e-mails that can be answered in three minutes or less. Choose two or three other times during the day when you can answer e-mails that need more attention.
- Deleting: If you read it and don't need it, delete it! Don't overthink it.
- Folders: Everything else goes into a folder. If e-mails can be answered today but need more time, put it in a folder and open that folder at your designated check-in time (other than opening and closing procedures).

*Here is one simple system that requires only **TEN** folders.*

INBOX: The inbox is a holding pen. E-mails shouldn't stay here any longer than it takes for you to file them into another folder. The exception to this rule is when you respond immediately and are waiting for an immediate response.

DO NOW: Everything that requires a response by end of the day.

MONDAY to FRIDAY: During designated work e-mail times, open the daily folder and begin responding. If by the end of Monday, there are still e-mails that aren't answered, move them to the folder when you are able to complete them. Do not leave them in that folder.

NEXT WEEK: Everything that requires a response by the end of next week.

THIS MONTH: Everything that needs a longer-term response. Depending on your role, you many need a monthly folder. Others can operate on a quarterly basis.

REFERENCE: If you often receive e-mails that are informational and will need to be easily accessed at some point, put them here. If you may need to reference an e-mail again, save it to this folder.

Be diligent

Once you embrace this system, you need to adhere to it diligently. We tend to get more lax about new systems as their newness rubs off, but if you stick to it, it will get easier and become more automatic. Be intentional about deleting e-mails that don't require your attention.

Five quick tips:

1 - **Keep an actual to-do list**. For example, if an e-mail thread results in deciding that you need to schedule a meeting, add it to your to-do list and delete the e-mail.
2 - **Don't exaggerate your own importance**. If you don't need to respond, put it in the reference folder or delete it—it's one or the other. And if you stay on 'cc,' you'll get the latest thread when everyone responds, so there's no need to worry.
3 - **Don't exaggerate the importance of others**. A lot of people want responses today. But not everyone needs a response today. Don't put e-mails in the *Today* folder that don't belong there; if it's in the *Today* folder, you have to respond to it today or move it to a different folder.

4 – **Project-based work**. If your work is project-based, you can create this ten-folder system for each project. After the project is complete, archive the entire structure.

Expect that this may feel awkward or even rigid at first. Expect that you may even justify that you can't possibly make this work. But you could try it as an experiment for a solid week and see if it begins to get easier as the week passes. There may be immediate stress in the beginning—that you are missing out on something or letting people down, but trust me . . . you were already doing both of those before; you just may not have known it. With this structure, you have the opportunity to be as effective as possible for yourself and your clients.

27

SUSTAINABILITY

You now have what it takes to think like an organized person, even if you still don't mind your somewhat (or very) messy desk. If you are still unsure if you have enough knowledge to access the tools that the organized thinker uses, let me put your mind at ease. You do!

You have all the knowledge you need, but it will take practice, consistency, and commitment to create change in a sustainable way. The sweet spot is in staying present on what is at hand, while knowing in the back of your mind what you want and what you don't want.

First, make a list of all the things you want to eliminate (examples)

- Clutter that makes me feel anxious.
- Constantly being late.
- Wasting time trying to find missing things.
- The feeling that I am running all day long.

Next, create a specific list of what you DO want (examples)

- Have a space for the things that matter to me.
- Be able to find my things easily.

- To feel calm and in control of my day.
- To be able to spend more time doing than thinking about what I need to do.
- The ability to feel completely present.
- The ability to focus for long periods of time on tasks that need it.
- To enjoy my life as it is, not yearning for the way I want it to be.

Once you have this list, you will be clear about your *why*. Without this, you will continue to resort to the way things were. The *why* is your prize. Always keep your eye on the prize.

I am not suggesting that because you have now read this book and can see the thought process of an organized person, that tomorrow you will suddenly awake with the same thinking process. You didn't get to this place in a night, and it will take a more than a few nights to create a new way of thinking, especially one that is sustainable.

But yes, you can do it! I have seen transformations over and over in my clients who have had enough of what is not working in their lives anymore. Successful people who had convinced themselves that the way it was was *good enough* even though it wasn't good at all. Successful people who were convinced that organization was in fact hereditary and that they simply weren't born with the clean-up gene. Yet it wasn't until they had had enough that they were willing to open their eyes to what might be possible.

As a result, I have witnessed amazing transformations as people committed to change. Because that is all we really need. A commitment to change and then some tools and understanding about what it takes to think like an organized person.

Literally, in several weeks' time, I have seen people's lives shift from being overwhelmed and stressed around a mess to thoughts surrounding careful and mindful placement of everyday matters. The sweet spot is to continue that shift until it becomes automatic. Until it becomes a way of life that actually feels natural.

The sweet spot is in the thought process. So yes, you do have it. You just need to access it. There needs to be a plan in place, which may involve reorganizing the way things are set up at the front door, at your desk, or even in the garage. It may take some time to create surroundings that foster your ability to be an organized thinker, but eventually it will be automatic and sustainable. A way of life. Imagine that!

Always ask yourself, "How can I compartmentalize this?"

Start with one topic at a time, beginning with the areas that would be most helpful to you right away. Once the space in that area is set up, let the games begin!

Be patient. But also be diligent!

Most importantly, remember that the best way to start anything is to simply begin.

ABOUT THE AUTHOR

Lesley Geller has been writing daily since the tender young age of nine, beginning her writing career in journals with a lock and key and eventually moving onto publishing on online platforms. Her first self-published book was *Own Your Now*, which was a compilation of the many blog articles she has written about life and work. She is inspired by the amazing professionals who challenge themselves while working with her as their business/life coach with Geller Coaching in order to tap into their true potential. That inspiration is what led her to write this book—in the hope of helping more successful professionals become as efficient, effective, and productive as they can be.

Geller Coaching has an intuitive style of coaching that enables individuals to attain the success they are capable of achieving by identifying obstacles and strengths to redefine what is possible. Successful professionals working with a coach experience sustainable change, as expectations of growth are exceeded and the next level of success is accomplished.

Geller lives in Yardley, PA with her husband and toy poodle. She enjoys spending time with her four children, daily journaling, blogging, running along the canal, and spending as much time as possible in Long Beach Island, relaxing under her umbrella with a book.

Interested in learning more about how having a business coach can take you to the next level? Visit the author's website at: www.GellerCoaching.com

www.ingramcontent.com/pod-product-compliance
Lightning Source LLC
Chambersburg PA
CBHW070240220526

45465CB00004B/1463